A fourth kind of exercise is the creative type, in which the student attempts to use from five to fifteen of the entry words of a unit in writing a paragraph on a topic suggested by the exercise. Pupils generally enjoy doing this kind of exercise. Such exercises are especially suitable for accelerated students. Yet slow students sometimes do an exercise of this type willingly and rather well.

## THE TESTING PROGRAM

The *Testing Program* is designed to complement the tests and the exercises in the text. The package of eighty duplicating masters includes the Diagnostic Test (discussed on page 4), forty Unit Tests, four Part Tests consisting, in all, of fifty-five sections, and six Crossword Exercises developed by a former student of *Word Wealth*.

The Unit Tests provide a final test for each of the forty units in the book. Each test, in the manner of the Second Practice Set in most units, covers the entry words and the related words. The advantage of these tests is that they require recognition of the word needed to convey a given meaning, but a student must often distinguish shades of meaning in a rather precise way.

The Part Tests cover entry words and related words in separate sections. If the Unit Tests prove too difficult for average or slow-learning groups, the teacher should use the Part Tests instead. A Part Test may be given as the final test after the three units that it covers have been studied. The teacher may use the entire test or only the sections covering entry words. Since the sections on related words are somewhat less difficult, however, than similar material in the Unit Tests, such sections should probably be attempted.

The complete *Testing Program* facilitates testing according to ability levels. The schedules that follow include information on how the *Testing Program* can be used for three different ability levels.

# SETTING A SCHEDULE

Some teachers like to spend two or three days a week on word work. Others prefer to spend fifteen or twenty minutes a day on a unit. For an average class, the two schedules will operate somewhat as follows:

## Average Class

**15-20 minutes a day**

**1st day:**
Pretest and six entry words with their variants and related words.
**2nd day:**
Fourteen entry words with variants and related words.
**3rd day:**
Give First Practice Set and grade it.
**4th day:**
Give Second Practice Set and grade it. Give Third Practice Set.
**5th day:**
Do an exercise or two and the Unit Test from the *Testing Program*.

**Two and one-half days a week**

**1st day:**
Do Pretest and cover entry words. Do First Practice Set and grade.
**2nd day:**
Do Second Practice Set and grade. Do Third Practice Set and grade.
**3rd day:**
Do Unit Test from the *Testing Program*. Or do Part Test on three units when these three have been completed.

## Accelerated Class Or Group

**15-20 minutes a day**

**1st day:**
Do Pretest and score it. Go over text, stressing the words and forms the class does not know. Cover related words.
**2nd day:**
Do Second and Third Practice Sets and grade them.
**3rd day:**
Do creative exercises, word games, and special projects.
**4th day:**
Do Unit Test.

**Two days per unit**

**1st day:**
Do Pretest and presentation of text. Do Second Practice Set.
**2nd day:**
Do Third Practice Set and grade it. Do creative exercises. Give Unit Test.

## Slow-Moving Class Or Group

**15-20 minutes a day**

**1st day:**
Do Pretest and score it. Go over four or five of the entry words and variant forms.
**2nd day:**
Go over seven or eight more entry words and variant forms.
**3rd day:**
Present the remaining entry words and variant forms.
**4th day:**
Do First Practice Set and score.
**5th day:**
Do part of depth studies and related words.
**6th day:**
Do more on related words and depth studies.
**7th day:**
Do one or two exercises from the text, especially word-building tabulations.
**8th day:**
Do Third Practice Set, if not too difficult, and perhaps another exercise.
**9th day:**
Do Second Practice Set and grade.
**10th day:**
Do Unit Test.

**Three or four days per week**

**1st day:**
Do Pretest and score it. Present half of the entry words in the Study Guide and their variant forms.
**2nd day:**
Work over the other ten entry words and their variant forms. Do a word-building exercise.
**3rd day:**
Do First Practice Set and grade it. Do Third Practice Set and grade it. Do one of the exercises, especially word building. Try Unit Test—or use three sections or all of appropriate Part Test when the three units it covers have been completed.
**4th day (optional):**
Do the related words and the Second Practice Set; but mastery of the entry words is more important than a hazy understanding of all the words. Unless a student is capable of readily grasping the subtle differences of meaning that are involved, including the Second Practice Set and the complete Unit Test is not recommended. Instead glean from the Unit Test those sentences based on the entry words only.

Thus a slow-moving class needs up to two weeks to do a unit thoroughly at the rate of 15—20 minutes per class session or at least three full days and preferably three and a half. It is suggested that a slow class or a slow-moving group in a class of mixed abilities cover only the entry words and variant forms. Thus, while the superior pupils do the entire unit, the slow class or group is expected to master only the entry words and their variants, do the First Practice Set, and the Third (if it is not the analogy type), and a part or all of the Unit Test at the teacher's discretion. In the Part Tests a slow class will do only the sections based on entry words.

The *Word Wealth* material lends itself well to a normal schedule of two units in a week once a month, especially during the months that are not interrupted by vacations or examinations. In this way a class would cover a minimum of ten units or one fourth of the book in a year or twenty units and one half of the book on an accelerated schedule. An accelerated group could conceivably cover the entire book in the eleventh grade or even in the tenth grade and thus be in a state of maximum readiness for the Scholastic Aptitude Test.

## GAMES AND CREATIVE DEPARTURES

Users of the book should not overlook the imaginative or unusual kinds of tests that may be devised. A cartoon quiz, for example, is one way of making tests creative. Objects or designs used in presenting the word may also be employed to comprise a test. Six crossword puzzles are provided in the *Testing Program* for this edition. Puzzles of this type also make good extra assignments for those students who have the skill and patience to compile them. An ingenious exercise in malapropisms makes a delightful "operation," and many of the words lend themselves to the game of charades.

Dozens of games, puzzles, and enjoyable activities that may be used to enliven word study are readily available. For certain groups these activities could conceivably replace the formal study of specific units, but their chief value is supplementary.

A good game for a listless class or a spare five minutes is called ECHOLALIA. The leader shouts a word like *spigot* and points at another pupil who, within ten seconds, must match it with a word of the same pattern, *i.e.*, the same number of syllables and the same ending. Thus *spigot* might produce *divot, pilot, riot, fagot,* etc.

One variation of this game is –(m)ony words. This game may be played with pencil-and-paper—duplicated (preferably) or read to the class.

1. Sounds like a bony knee: _____
2. Uses the name of the supreme being (Moslem): _____
3. Injurious at first: _____
4. Stocks at face value: _____
5. Begins with an examination: _____
6. Uses a woman's name: _____
7. Uses a relative: _____
8. Father plus oak: _____
9. His last name was Barjesus: _____
10. A sharp one: _____

**Answers**

1. *ebony*
2. *alimony (Allah)*
3. *harmony*
4. *parsimony*
5. *testimony*
6. *ceremony (Sarah)*
7. *antimony (Auntie)*
8. *patrimony (tree)*
9. *simony*
10. *acrimony*

–Shun Words will make an oral challenge game that can go on indefinitely, but it will be more challenging and more instructive if each response is limited to two syllables or to the same root + –tion or –sion that the leader used. The next leader may shift to a different root, and the game can become quite a comprehensive review of word elements, using such groups as these:

| | | |
|---|---|---|
| diction | induction | confusion |
| fiction | deduction | profusion |
| friction | reduction | effusion |
| fraction | conduction | diffusion |
| faction | production | infusion |
| | | |
| contention | proposition | institution |
| detention | imposition | restitution |
| retention | deposition | constitution |
| pretension | supposition | destitution |
| extension | apposition | prostitution |

This game lends itself well to a duplicated written test, thus:

1. Quacker at sea: _____
2. You ride a wreck: _____
3. Vacation for two: _____
4. Pay by the dish: _____
5. To bury a maiden: _____
6. A pen speaks: _____
7. To stimulate by burial: _____
8. Faint light just created: _____
9. Smells bad: _____
10. Nine plus one = : _____

**Answers**

1. *seduction (sea duck)*
2. *injunction*
3. *restitution*
4. *perdition*
5. *intermission*
6. *dispensation*
7. *interspersion*
8. *dimunition*
9. *extinction*
10. *tension*

The same kind of game with its three variations may be planed with –sive Words:

1. A heavy one: _____
2. An inactive one: _____
3. Come running, or write: _____
4. Hard to catch: _____
5. Deceptive, unreal: _____
6. Encouraging one: _____
7. Violating privacy: _____
8. Too much outgo: _____
9. Like a clique: _____
10. Makes fun of you: _____

**Answers**

1. *massive*
2. *passive*
3. *cursive*
4. *elusive*
5. *delusive*
6. *conducive*
7. *intrusive*
8. *effusive*
9. *exclusive*
10. *derisive*

Three similar games may be devised from the –ate words: *temperate, satiate, retaliate, (de)liberate, appreciate, validate,* etc. –Al words offer another set of games, and the supply of examples is almost inexhaustible: *pastoral, temporal, territorial, mercurial, infernal,* etc. –City words offer adequate material for still another set of challenge, quiz, or puzzle items: *perspicacity, duplicity, complicity, audacity, eccentricity, rapacity, reciprocity,* and many others, including everyday words like *capacity, electricity,* and *loquacity.* –Able words like *capable* augment the list.

Prefixes are as suitable as suffixes for the games suggested above, except that in– words and un– words are almost too numerous to be interesting or challenging in such a game. Meta– words, on the other hand, are scarcely numerous enough and are often too technical. The Latin prepositions generally and perhaps the a– (no) words of Greek origin are interesting possibilities. Number prefixes, especially the first three, present possibilities, but the uses of others are not so numerous as one would think. The advantage of prefixes is that one can quickly round up most of the available examples in a dictionary.

A word game called STRIP TEASE is another instructive pastime. In playing it the leader proposes a word like *adverse* and calls on someone to strip off a letter leaving a viable word. A penalty must be paid if the pupil cannot do it—provided the leader can. Thus the leader must make sure that the word proposed can be stripped down letter by letter or two letters at a time to a residual two-letter word. The word *adverse* may be stripped as follows: *adverse, averse, verse, Erse, ere,* and *re.*

Another type of game which two pupils can play with each other or which a larger group can enjoy is called the TWILIGHT ZONE or the WORD FARTHEST OUT. The leader challenges another pupil with a word to define. If the pupil cannot define it and the leader can, the pupil loses a point. The pupil who satisfactorily defines the word becomes the leader. Naturally each person in the group offers the most difficult word that he or she can command.

This kind of game is likely to lead sooner or later to WORDS RARELY SEEN. To play it well one must jot down dozens of unfamiliar words wherever they may be found and even ransack the dictionary for them. Here are a few, all interesting, but almost unknown.

**novercal**   of or like a stepmother: Mrs. Burwell plays a *novercal* role in the Orcutt family.

**helotry**   serfdom or slavery: Prime Minister Harold Wilson once warned England of "an industrial *helotry* under which we in Europe produce only the conventional apparatus of a modern economy while becoming increasingly dependent on American business for sophisticated apparatus which will call the tune in the 70's and 80's." (*Query:* Elicit from the students their opinion as to whether Wilson's prediction has come true.)

**tumescent**   swelling, becoming swollen: *Tumescent* feet are a symptom of dropsy.

**crassitude**   ignorance, stupidity: George displayed surprising *crassitude* in his business dealings.

**erubescent**    reddish, blushing, turning red: Cherries become *erubescent* as they ripen.

**steatopygia**    fatty enlargement of the hips: *Steatopygia* afflicts many car-borne Americans.

**ophiolatry**    the worship of snakes: *Ophiolatry* persists in certain areas of the world.

**levoduction**    leftward motion, as of the eye: Socialistic *levoduction* spread across Europe.

**desquamation**    the peeling off of scales: *Desquamation* of fish is a tiresome chore.

**duodenary**    increasing by twelves, having to do with twelves: The celebration is a *duodenary* event.

If the game of WORDS RARELY SEEN ever palls or runs dry—which is most unlikely—one resource beyond it is the game of WHAT WOULD IT MEAN? This game proposes words that are hypothetical, that have perhaps been used or perhaps have just been coined and in either case must be defined without benefit of a dictionary. Here one must fall back on the meanings of word elements, on analogy, on common sense, and finally on sheer temerity. Only the most intrepid minds dare to venture into this realm of hypothecation or have the pitons and other Alpine equipment required for such hazardous adventures. To begin, remind your students of the various ways words can enter a language: by clipping (cutting an old word short in front or in back or otherwise abbreviating it); by compounding; by outright borrowing from other languages (as the current *ciao* from Italian); by inventing new meanings for old words (as *angel* for radar echo); by the evil abduction of trade marks (a lawless practice); by sheer invention or lucky happenstance. G. & C. Merriam Company's *6,000 Words, A Supplement to Webster's Third New International Dictionary* (Springfield, Massachusetts, 1976), lists those recent words that have appeared in print sufficiently often to warrant official dictionary recognition. Among the entries cited are *flashcube, pulsars, nonperson, boatel* (boat plus hotel); *waterbed; parajournalism; mailgram; antianxiety; teach-in; chugalug; pantsuit; underwhelm*. The fun of word creation could lead your more advanced students to such questions as the following:

1. Would it be possible to *aridify* water?

2. What would *lividity* be?

3. If *anecdotage* is a disease of old age, what is a *seniliar*? An *alludascope*?

4. What would a *monogon* be? a *centagon*? a *logophile*? a *semilateral* action? a *fratriarch*?

5. Would an *antiloquent* huckster or politician prove persuasive, or is it a word to describe television fans fed up with obtrusive advertising?

*16/Introduction*

A contest to see who can name the longest word is always exhilarating, at least if *disestablishmentarianism* is proscribed at the outset. Such words as the following will then begin to vie with each other:

apprehensiveness (five syllables, 16 letters)
mononucleosis (six, 13 letters)
incompatibility (seven, 15 letters)
imperturbability (seven, 16 letters)
ultraconservativeness (seven, 21 letters)
incomprehensibility (eight, 19 letters)
counterrevolutionary (eight, 20 letters)
antiparliamentarianism (ten, 22 letters)

*Antidisestablishmentarianism,* with its eleven syllables and 28 letters, would still win if it were admissible in the competition. A lake in Massachusetts has a name which is longer, however: Chargoggagoggmanchauggaguggchaubunagungamaugg. It has 14 syllables and 45 letters.

Two extra word puzzles follow.

## All's Well That Ends OK*

Take a good look at the definitions on the right and fill in the missing letters in the words on the left.

1.  __ __ OK            frenzied
2.  __ __ OK            register
3.  __ __ OK            trap
4.  __ __ OK            defraud
5.  __ __ __ OK         tolerate
6.  __ __ __ OK         bend
7.  __ __ __ OK         swayed
8.  __ __ __ OK         hobgoblin
9.  __ __ __ __ OK      loose
10. __ __ __ __ __ OK   warm wind
11. __ __ __ __ __ OK   abandoned
12. __ __ __ __ __ OK   apprehended wrongly
13. __ __ __ __ __ OK   prospect
14. __ __ __ __ __ __ OK   neglect
15. __ __ __ __ __ __ OK   variety of muslin

**Answers**

| | | | |
|---|---|---|---|
| 1. *amok* | 5. *brook* | 9. *unhook* | 13. *outlook* |
| 2. *book* | 6. *crook* | 10. *chinook* | 14. *overlook* |
| 3. *hook* | 7. *shook* | 11. *forsook* | 15. *nainsook* |
| 4. *rook* | 8. *spook* | 12. *mistook* | |

*Compiled by Fannie Gross for *Saturday Review,* December 16, 1961. Reprinted by permission.

## Triple Threat*

The Greeks had a word for it; the Romans had a word for it; the Anglo-Saxons had a word for it. And that is why when, in English, we can either foretell, or predict, or prophesy, it's the Anglo-Saxon, the Latin, and the Greek for it. In the group of "triplets" below, supply the missing word in each set (one blank represents one letter).

| Anglo-Saxon | Latin | Greek |
|---|---|---|
| 1. fellow-feeling | _ _ _ _ _ _ _ _ _ | sympathy |
| 2. many-tongued | multilingual | _ _ _ _ _ _ _ _ |
| 3. _ _ _ _ _ _ | occult | cryptic |
| 4. beginner | _ _ _ _ _ _ | neophyte |
| 5. old | antique | _ _ _ _ _ _ _ |
| 6. _ _ _ _ _ _ _ | frugal | economical |
| 7. forecast | _ _ _ _ _ _ _ | prognosticate |
| 8. forsaker | defector | _ _ _ _ _ _ _ _ |
| 9. _ _ _ _ | conversation | dialogue |
| 10. angry | _ _ _ _ _ | choleric |
| 11. teamwork | cooperation | _ _ _ _ _ _ _ |
| 12. _ _ _ | adversary | antagonist |
| 13. fleeting | _ _ _ _ _ _ _ _ _ _ | ephemoral |
| 14. rift | division | _ _ _ _ _ _ |
| 15. _ _ _ _ _ _ _ | adore | idolize |

### Answers

1. *compassion*
2. *polyglot*
3. *hidden*
4. *novice*
5. *archaic*
6. *thrifty*
7. *predict*
8. *apostate*
9. *talk*
10. *irate*
11. *synergy*
12. *foe*
13. *evanescent*
14. *schism*
15. *worship*

*Compiled by Morris Rosenblum and Maxwell Nurnberg for *Saturday Review*, January 2, 1965. Reprinted by permission.

# KEYS FOR: WORD WEALTH TESTING PROGRAM

Keys for Diagnostic Test, Part Tests, and Crossword Exercises follow; keys for the Unit Tests appear with the Teacher's Guide materials for each unit.

## DIAGNOSTIC TEST

### Entry Words

|    | 1/A | 1/B | 1/C | 2/A | 2/B | 2/C |
|----|-----|-----|-----|-----|-----|-----|
| 1. | g   | b   | i   | e   | e   | e   |
| 2. | j   | g   | e   | g   | h   | h   |
| 3. | f   | e   | a   | a   | j   | g   |
| 4. | a   | c   | g   | b   | a   | b   |
| 5. | h   | i   | b   | j   | b   | i   |
| 6. | d   | d   | d   | i   | i   | a   |
| 7. | e   | h   | h   | c   | c   | c   |
| 8. | b   | f   | f   | d   | f   | j   |
| 9. |     | j   |     |     |     | k   |

|    | 3/A | 3/B | 3/C | 4/A | 4/B | 4/C |
|----|-----|-----|-----|-----|-----|-----|
| 1. | i   | g   | b   | h   | e   | d   |
| 2. | f   | e   | f   | c   | c   | i   |
| 3. | a   | i   | e   | f   | h   | f   |
| 4. | g   | a   | j   | a   | b   | j   |
| 5. | b   | b   | a   | j   | d   | a   |
| 6. | d   | j   | h   | d   | a   | b   |
| 7. | j   | c   | c   | b   | i   | c   |
| 8. | e   | f   | i   | e   | g   | e   |
| 9. |     | d   |     |     | k   |     |

### Related Words

|     | A | B | C | D | E |
|-----|---|---|---|---|---|
| 1.  | h | d | j | i | d |
| 2.  | e | f | e | h | h |
| 3.  | j | j | h | d | k |
| 4.  | l | a | f | a | b |
| 5.  | a | i | b | k | g |
| 6.  | i | c | a | l | a |
| 7.  | f | b | l | b | i |
| 8.  | b | l | k | j | f |
| 9.  | g | g | c | e | j |
| 10. | d | e | g | c | l |

# PART TESTS   PART ONE

| Section 1 | Section 2 | Section 3 | Section 4 | Section 5 |
|---|---|---|---|---|
| 1. e | h | b | d | g |
| 2. h | e | d | i | f |
| 3. a | d | i | g | k |
| 4. k | j | f | a | a |
| 5. l | i | c | c | h |
| 6. g | k | a | k | l |
| 7. b | f | j | j | e |
| 8. f | c | e | b | j |
| 9. j | b | g | h | c |
| 10. i | l | k | l | d |

| Section 6 | Section 7 | Section 8 | Section 9 | Section 10 |
|---|---|---|---|---|
| 1. e | l | j | k | d |
| 2. c | d | e | g | i |
| 3. f | i | h | a | h |
| 4. a | b | c | b | f |
| 5. h | c | i | h | b |
| 6. j | j | a | l | a |
| 7. i | e | k | c | k |
| 8. g | f | d | j | g |
| 9. k | h | g | e | l |
| 10. d | a | f | f | c |

| Section 11 | Section 12 | Section 13 | Section 14 | Section 15 |
|---|---|---|---|---|
| 1. c | d | c | c | g |
| 2. d | h | e | i | a |
| 3. e | g | h | e | d |
| 4. i | a | d | k | k |
| 5. a | i | a | j | i |
| 6. f | l | g | a | l |
| 7. g | k | i | l | b |
| 8. k | j | l | f | f |
| 9. j | f | j | b | e |
| 10. b | c | b | g | h |

# PART TESTS  PART TWO

| Section 1 | Section 2 | Section 3 | Section 4 | Section 5 |
|---|---|---|---|---|
| 1. j | d | l | i | d |
| 2. d | j | a | a | h |
| 3. f | e | e | l | k |
| 4. k | f | j | b | b |
| 5. b | i | d | d | i |
| 6. a | l | g | j | j |
| 7. i | a | b | h | e |
| 8. l | b | k | k | a |
| 9. g | h | f | g | l |
| 10. h | g | c | e | g |

| Section 6 | Section 7 | Section 8 | Section 9 | Section 10 |
|---|---|---|---|---|
| 1. i | e | g | c | j |
| 2. f | k | h | j | g |
| 3. a | j | i | f | l |
| 4. c | b | c | a | b |
| 5. h | c | k | l | f |
| 6. j | l | a | k | c |
| 7. d | h | d | b | k |
| 8. k | i | e | g | d |
| 9. b | d | j | e | h |
| 10. e | a | l | h | e |

| Section 11 | Section 12 | Section 13 | Section 14 | Section 15 |
|---|---|---|---|---|
| 1. b | d | k | f | b |
| 2. d | h | i | d | f |
| 3. f | l | b | k | j |
| 4. c | g | j | g | a |
| 5. k | a | f | b | k |
| 6. e | k | h | i | g |
| 7. h | j | a | l | c |
| 8. g | b | e | c | d |
| 9. l | f | l | e | h |
| 10. i | e | g | h | l |

# PART TESTS    PART THREE

| Section 1 | Section 2 | Section 3 | Section 4 | Section 5 |
|---|---|---|---|---|
| 1. f | k | h | c | l |
| 2. k | g | f | i | h |
| 3. h | l | e | k | d |
| 4. g | c | j | l | a |
| 5. j | i | k | j | j |
| 6. a | b | b | e | k |
| 7. i | j | l | b | c |
| 8. d | e | a | d | i |
| 9. l | d | c | f | b |
| 10. b | f | i | h | f |

| Section 6 | Section 7 | Section 8 | Section 9 | Section 10 |
|---|---|---|---|---|
| 1. c | g | g | b | k |
| 2. k | i | h | l | e |
| 3. f | h | f | j | a |
| 4. h | f | a | f | i |
| 5. j | a | l | d | c |
| 6. i | b | b | k | j |
| 7. a | d | d | g | f |
| 8. d | k | i | h | l |
| 9. g | l | e | e | g |
| 10. e | e | c | c | h |

| Section 11 | Section 12 | Section 13 | Section 14 | Section 15 |
|---|---|---|---|---|
| 1. h | j | b | d | l |
| 2. c | a | c | a | d |
| 3. i | b | a | j | i |
| 4. a | g | e | g | a |
| 5. l | c | g | i | h |
| 6. d | i | l | c | k |
| 7. f | e | i | l | e |
| 8. k | f | h | k | g |
| 9. b | h | j | b | f |
| 10. j | l | k | f | c |

# PART TESTS  PART FOUR

| Section 1 | Section 2 | Section 3 | Section 4 | Section 5 |
|---|---|---|---|---|
| 1. h | e | k | c | f |
| 2. a | i | d | e | d |
| 3. f | a | f | i | j |
| 4. l | k | a | g | l |
| 5. j | d | i | k | b |
| 6. c | g | b | a | i |
| 7. b | l | l | j | k |
| 8. d | b | g | d | c |
| 9. g | j | e | f | g |
| 10. e | c | h | h | h |

| Section 6 | Section 7 | Section 8 | Section 9 | Section 10 |
|---|---|---|---|---|
| 1. j | e | e | b | k |
| 2. e | j | i | a | l |
| 3. a | h | b | g | d |
| 4. h | l | k | l | h |
| 5. l | b | j | d | a |
| 6. d | c | l | i | i |
| 7. c | a | c | k | e |
| 8. i | d | f | j | j |
| 9. b | g | g | f | b |
| 10. f | i | h | h | f |

# CROSSWORD EXERCISES

## Number 1

# Number II

|   | T | R | A | N | S | M | U | T | E |   | M | I | R | A | G | E |   |   | C |
|---|---|---|---|---|---|---|---|---|---|---|---|---|---|---|---|---|---|---|---|
|   |   | E |   | E |   | O |   |   |   |   | M |   | V | E | R | T | I | G | O |
|   | E | N | I | G | M | A |   | F |   |   | P |   |   |   |   | N | O | N |   |
|   |   | O |   | A |   | N | E | B | U | L | O | U | S |   | S |   | F |   |   |
| D | U | E | T |   |   |   |   | R |   |   | T |   | U |   | E |   |   |   |   |
|   |   | N |   | E |   | E | D | I | T |   | E |   | C |   | C | R | Y | O |   |
|   |   | C |   | X |   |   |   | V |   |   |   |   | C |   | I |   |   | B |   |
| S | E | N | I | L | E |   |   | E |   | O | B | N | O | X | I | O | U | S |   |
|   |   |   |   | E |   |   |   |   |   |   | T |   | R |   | R |   |   | T |   |
| L | A | T | E | N | T |   |   |   |   |   | T |   | A |   |   |   |   | R |   |
|   |   | A |   | I |   | A | R | B | O | R |   | C | R | U | S | A | D | E |   |
| F |   | N |   | O |   | R |   |   |   | U |   | I |   |   | G |   |   | P |   |
| L | E | G | I | O | N |   | S |   |   | S |   | T |   | M | I | S | C | E |   |
| A |   |   |   |   |   | O | B | S | T | I | N | A | T | E |   |   |   | R |   |
| G |   | J | A | R | G | O | N |   |   | V |   | D |   | N | E | C | R | O |   |
| R |   | C |   |   |   | V | E | H | E | M | E | N | T |   | H |   |   | U |   |
| A | M | B | U | S | H |   | E |   | E |   | O | L |   |   | I |   |   | S |   |
| N |   | T |   |   |   |   | N |   | R |   | N |   |   |   | R |   |   |   |   |
| T | E | N | E | T | S |   | H | E | T | E | R | O | G | E | N | E | O | U | S |

## Number III

## Number IV

| | |1 I| |2 C|3 S|T|O|D|Y| |4 C|O|G|5 N|
|---|---|---|---|---|---|---|---|---|---|---|---|---|---|---|
| | |N|6 A| |T| | | |7 I| | | | |A|
| | |8 F|R|U|S|T|R|A|9 T|E| |10 N|O|M|11 A|D|
| | |E| D| | |A| |O| | |C| |E| |I|
| | |R| A| | |T| |O| |12 M|I|R|R|O|R|
| | |I| |13 C|O|V|E|T| | |S| |G| | |
| | |O| I| | |G| |14 M|15 A|N|I|F|E|S|16 T|
| |17 R|O|T|18 A|R|Y| |E|19 V| | | | | |E|
| | | |Y| E| |20 D|E|M|E|A|21 N|O|R|
| | | |22 D| |C| |L| |E| |U| |R|
|23 F|U|24 G|I|T|I|V|E| |S| | |R| |I|
|E| |E| O| | | |Y| |I| |25 T|O|T|
|26 I|G|N|27 O|R|E| | | |S| |U| |O|
|G| |S| | |28 U| |29 E|R|R|O|R|
|30 N|O|N|C|H|A|L|A|N|C|E| |E| |Y|

# Number V

## Number VI

|   | 1 E | X | 2 T | R | I | 3 C | A | T | 4 E |   | 5 A | P | P | 6 A | L | L |   | 7 C | H | 8 I |
|---|---|---|---|---|---|---|---|---|---|---|---|---|---|---|---|---|---|---|---|---|

(crossword grid — solution as filled)

Across/Down answers visible in grid:

- 1 EXTRICATE
- 4 APPALL
- 6 CHI / CHIN (C-H-I then column)
- 8 UNITE
- 9 EPOCH
- 10 MARATHON
- 11 EMINENT
- 12 BRUSQUE
- 15 GRAV...
- 16 AUDIBLE
- 17 SANCT
- 18 COUNSEL
- 21 NEGLIGIBLE
- 23 BREVITY
- 25 UN
- 26 REPRIMAND
- 29 GRASP
- 32 POLIT
- 33 YORE
- 34 AGILE
- 36 DROLL
- 39 EPICURE
- 41 CANDID
- 46 ROTOR
- 48 FIEND
- 49 DIVERGE
- 50 PONE
- 51 REVERIE

Down fills include: EXUBERANT, RETENTION, EXORCISE, USURP, QUASI, LAX, CON, GRAVE, INNOVATOR, SACRAMENT, CEASE, SLATTERN, LITIGATE, VIA, URN, CACOPHONY, UNRULY, DEFRAY, ACCEDE, GRUDGE, PROMULGATE, ERG, APOSTROPHE, LITHE, AI, RIOT, SUQUITE, LEQUITE...

(Number VI crossword puzzle, fully solved)

# part one

## unit one

### WORD CHOICE

| | | | | |
|---|---|---|---|---|
| 1. divulge | 2. implore | 3. adapt | 4. affirm | 5. curtail |
| 6. acquire | 7. coerce | 8. defer | 9. admonish | 10. abolish |

### VERBS

**1. abolish**

*Eradicate* and its variants come from the Latin e– plus *radix, radicis,* root, and thus the literal meaning is to pull out by the roots. To *expunge* something, usually a written record of some kind, is to wipe it out or strike it out, as if with a sponge, but the root *pungere* means to strike or prick.

**2. acquire**

The root is the Latin verb *quaerere,* to seek. List other –quir– words, such as *inquire, inquiry; require, requirement; query, quest.*

**3. adapt**

Compare *adjust, conform, accommodate, harmonize.*

**4. admonish**

Both *forewarn* and *forebode* are typical words of Old English derivation, the combining form fore– meaning occurring beforehand; prior in rank, time, or place. Other fore– words include *forearm, foreleg, forecast, forehead, forehanded, forego.* (For– in such words as *forbear, forbid, forgo, forget* is a prefix meaning away, so as to involve exclusion or neglect.)

**5. affirm**

Adjective forms *declarative* and *negative* may be added. Point out the un– forms that are available: *undeclared, unwarranted, undeniable, unavowed, unrepudiated.*

**6. coerce**

It derives from the Latin co–, together, plus *arcere,* to confine. Compare *incarcerate,* from the Latin *carcer,* prison.

## 7. curtail

The word, altered by association with *tail*, comes from *curtal*, which once meant a horse with a "docked" or shortened tail. *Curtal* in turn comes from the Latin *curtus*, short. To *truncate* means to shorten, especially a line of poetry. To *desiccate* is to dry up: California was desiccated by the drought.

## 8. defer

List other –fer words such as *confer, infer, offer, prefer, refer*.

## 9. divulge

Antonyms of *divulge* include *conceal, hide, secrete,* and *cache*, though *cache* is usually a noun.

## 10. implore

List other –plore– words such as *deplore, explore, explorative, exploration*. The root meaning is to bewail or lament.

# NOUNS

## 1. ambush

The word is both a noun and a verb (see examples). *Ambush* comes from Latin in– plus *boscus*, woods. Compare the Australian use of *bush* for the wilderness. *Bois* is French for park.

## 2. contour

A *contour* map is a series of very irregular concentric circles. The word may be traced to the Greek *tornos*, a tool for making a circle.

## 3. guile

Compare *beguile*, to cheat, deceive, amuse, pass time pleasantly.

## 4. jargon

*Flapdoodle* (food for fools) is a particularly satisfying, though colloquial, term for wordy nonsense. *Gobbledygook* is the more modern synonym. *Verbiage* is a good word for the mere amassing of words.

## 5. labyrinth

Mary Renault's novel, *The King Must Die*, tells a captivating story of Theseus and his team of bull dancers who finally "liberated" the labyrinth and overthrew King Minos. Thus they relieved Athens of its obligation to send a shipload of young people to King Minos as a sacrifice each year. Ariadne, the daughter of King Minos, was the one who gave Theseus the thread by which he found his way out of the labyrinth.

6. **medley**

   Along with *meddle* it has been traced back to the Latin verb *miscere*, to mix (see –misce– WW p. 352).

7. **rapture**

   A person *enamored* is captivated, delighted, in love with the object or activity named, but the word carries just a hint of disparagement or disapproval. *Infatuation* has an even greater flavor of being deceived or ill-advised. Antonyms include *sorrow, pain, dejection, anguish, heartache. Rapture* comes from the Latin *rapere*, to seize, *rhapsody* from the Greek word *rhapsōidos*, one who strings songs together or who recites epic poetry.

8. **robot**

   Mention *automat*, a coin-in-the-slot restaurant (currently on the verge of extinction); *automation*, the process of making machines do more and more of the work human beings once did; and *automatic*.

9. **verge**

   The noun form comes from *virga*, a Latin word for a stick, rod, or wand. The *verger* is a person who carries the staff of office in an ecclesiastical procession —or more often the man who takes care of the interior of a church or cathedral.

10. **zephyr**

    *Zephyr* cloth is a thin, soft material for women's clothing, like cashmere. The mythological name of the north wind or wind from the mountains is *Boreas*. Other wind words include *gale, blast, windstorm, whirlwind, cyclone, tornado, hurricane* (*typhoon* in Asia), *monsoon* (reversible, seasonal wind and heavy rains of the Indian Ocean and southeast Asia), *simoom* (hot, violent desert wind or sandstorm), *tempest*.

# KEYS

**First Practice Set**

1. jargon, abolishing
2. adapted, acquire
3. ambush, curtail
4. zephyrs, medley
5. admonished, robot
6. affirmative, divulge
7. implored, guile
8. coerce, defer
9. labyrinth, verge
10. rapture, contour

## Second Practice Set

1. supplicate, annul
2. constrain, entreat
3. exposure, revelation
4. gobbledygook, warrant
5. profile, enchanting
6. heterogeneous, importune
7. vernacular, fustian
8. enthralled, entranced
9. cant, camouflage
10. alloy, extort

## Third Practice Set

1. c (readily adjustable)
2. e (warning)
3. d (gentle, breezy)
4. b (cancellation)
5. d (having intricate paths)
6. d (deceit)
7. b (delay)
8. c (specialized language)
9. d (refined delight)
10. c (declare)

## Antonyms

1. b (expend)
2. a (downcast)
3. c (deny)
4. d (deceitful)
5. a (conceal)
6. a (importune)
7. e (increase)
8. e (object to)
9. d (plain language)
10. a (tornado)

# UNIT TEST   *(Word Wealth Testing Program)*

1. e (acquisition);   x (defer)
2. t (coerce);   s (curtail)
3. z (extort);   v (abolish)
4. q (warrant);   a (admonition)
5. j (guile);   y (annul)
6. o (affirm);   u (divulge);   w (implore)
7. r (constrain);   b (disestablishment)
8. g (ambush);   n (verge)
9. h (labyrinth);   l (revelation)
10. d (robot);   k (enhancement)
11. f (gobbledygook);   m (gusto)
12. i (miscellany);   c (rapture)

# unit two

## THE RIGHT WORD

1. esteem  2. salvage  3. redeem  4. counsel  5. custody  6. appall
7. deluge  8. obsess  9. cherish  10. chaos  11. wrest  12. citadel

## VERBS

1. **apall**

    The root is a– plus *pale* from the Latin *pallere,* to be pale. It should not be confused with *pall* (a gloomy covering like clouds or smoke, or a dark cloth to cover a coffin) from the Latin *pallium*. But *pall* (to satiate, disgust, become wearisome) comes from the Middle English word *appallen,* to appall.

2. **discern**

    *Concern, concerning,* and *concernment* also comes from the Latin root *cernere,* to separate, to sift.

3. **esteem**

    *Estimate, estimation, estimator, estimative* come from the same Latin root, *estimare,* to appraise, set a value on.

4. **feign**

    *Figment* (something imagined) comes from the same root, the Latin verb *fingere,* to give shape to. Some authorities trace *fiction* to this root. The word *finger,* however, has been traced to a series of words meaning five.

5. **meditate**

    Other related words include *calculate* (to think in a mathematical sense); *lucubrate* (to think by lamplight). Hawthorne in the preface to *The Scarlet Letter* speaks of the "moth-eaten *lucubrations* of Mr. Surveyor Pue." *Cerebration,* a word for mental activity in its more mechanical-electrical sense, is often used humorously.

## 6. obsess

From its root, *sedere*, to sit, come *sedentary, sedate, sedan, sedative, sedation*. Like *obsess*, the word *session* (a sitting) comes from the past participle of *sedere*. But note that words like *concession* and *procession* come from –<u>cede</u>–, –<u>cess</u>– (WW p. 279) and not from *sedere* or *sessus*.

## 7. redeem

The word *Redeemer*, usually used with a capital letter, is an epithet of Christ. *Deem* (to believe, judge) in such sentences as "I did not *deem* it wise to go" comes from the Old English word *deman*, to doom; whereas *redeem* comes from the Latin <u>re</u>–, back, again, plus *emere*, to get or buy.

## 8. relent

*Lento* (slow), *lentando* (slower by degrees), and *lentissimo* (very slowly) come from the same Latin root *lentus*, which in *relent* has more the meaning of soft or flexible.

## 9. salvage

Note that the –<u>able</u> form retains the final *e* to keep the *g* sound soft as in *knowledgeable, manageable*, and other such words. Related words from the Latin *salvus*, safe, include *salute* and its variants; and *salvo* (volley of guns or burst of applause).

## 10. wrest

One of the few entry words in this book that comes from Old English. The root is *wraestan*, to twist violently. *Wrist* and *wrestle* derive from the same root, and *wrench* is related, having the same hypothetical word in Indo-European as its ultimate source.

# NOUNS

## 1. brevity

Synonyms include *terseness* and *succinctness* (WW p. 205). *Laconic* is an entry word on p. 163 of *Word Wealth*.

## 2. censure

The Latin root *censere*, to tax, evaluate, judge, is also the source of *censor, censurable, censorship, censorious*, and *census*. Shakespeare wrote in Polonius' advice to Laertes: "Take each man's censure, but reserve thy judgment."

3. **chaos**

   An *indiscriminate* or *promiscuous* heap of objects is *chaotic*, but *promiscuity* usually indicates moral irregularity or chaos. The word *chaos* is a Greek word imported through Latin into English. It in turn may be traced to the Greek verb from which *chasm* derives.

4. **citadel**

   This word comes by way of a French and an earlier Italian word from the Latin *civitas*, citizenship. Pupils may cite additional examples of a citadel, both literal and figurative.

5. **counsel**

   Add *counselor* as a variant. *Consul* comes from the same Latin source, as well as its variants, *consular, consulate, consulship*. So do *consult, consultant, consultation, consultative*.

6. **celebrity**

   From its Latin root *celeber*, frequented, populous, come also *celebrate, celebrant, celebration, celebrator*. *Celibate* (unmarried) has quite a different Latin root, caelib–, caelebs, akin to Old English *libban*, to live.

7. **custody**

   Add *custodial, custodianship*, but not *custom* or any of its variants.

8. **deluge**

   *Postdiluvian* society was that which existed after the Flood. From the Latin root *luere*, to wash, comes *ablution(s)* (act of washing the hands or body). Include *inundation* as a synonym of *deluge*.

9. **demeanor**

   One's *bearing* and especially one's *carriage* connote posture and physical qualities, whereas *demeanor* refers primarily to one's attitude or spirit.

10. **epoch**

    The root is Greek. Other "epoch" words include *decade, century, era, millennium, reign*, also such adjectival phrases as *ante-bellum* fashions or *Empire* furniture.

# KEYS

**First Practice Set**

1. celebrity, brevity
2. esteem, deluge
3. counsel, feign
4. discern, obsess
5. chaos, appall
6. epoch, relent
7. censure, wrest
8. meditate, citadel
9. salvage, demeanor
10. custody, redeem

**Second Practice Set**

| | A. | B. |
|---|---|---|
| 1. | 12 | 3 |
| 2. | 8 | 7 |
| 3. | 5 | 11 |
| 4. | 2 | 2 |
| 5. | 10 | 4 |
| 6. | 6 | 6 |
| 7. | 9 | 1 |
| 8. | 4 | 12 |
| 9. | 7 | 5 |
| 10. | 1 | 8 |

**A Word for It**

1. homage
2. esteem
3. censorious
4. ruminate
5. ponder
6. feint
7. cherish
8. retrospection
9. harassment
10. rehabilitate

## UNIT TEST  *(Word Wealth Testing Program)*

1. d (havoc);  q (obsess)
2. w (discern);  g (disarray);  a (derangement)
3. u (feign);  h (esteem)
4. r (appall);  z (deliberate)
5. x (cherish);  k (homage)
6. m (citadel);  j (epoch)
7. s (relent);  b (pandemonium)
8. o (celebrity);  c (custody)
9. y (inundate);  e (contemplation)
10. p (ruminate);  i (retrospection)
11. v (conceive);  t (redeem)
12. f (brevity);  l (censure)

# unit three

## TRAITS

1. b (stern, gloomy)
2. d (mournful)
3. c (clear)
4. a (thoughtful)
5. d (frank)
6. b (appearing reasonable)
7. c (stealthy)
8. b (excessively fat)
9. a (hazy)
10. c (powerful)

## ADJECTIVES

1. **brusque**

   The word is French, from an Italian word derived probably from *bruscus*, brushwood, in Medieval Latin, and this in turn from the Latin word *ruscus*, broom.

2. **candid**

   The root *candidus* (white, sincere) from which this word comes is derived in turn from the Latin verb *candere*, to glow or shine. *Candidate* (white-robed), *candle, incandescent,* and the name *Candide* come from the same Latin verb. Antonyms include *disingenuous*.

3. **delinquent**

   Though *delinquency* denotes merely a shortcoming or failure, it is used now for positive antisocial or criminal actions.

4. **dour**

   The word comes from the Latin adjective *durus*, hard, from which come *durable* and its variants, *duress, endure,* and *obdurate*.

5. **obese**

   The word comes from the Latin *obesus*, having devoured, presumably, too much food.

6. **furtive**

   *Covert, clandestine, underhanded,* and sometimes *subtle* are approximate synonyms. *Overt, open,* and *unconcealed* are antonyms.

## 7. lucid

*Pellucid* is an older, more intense, and more literary word used with similar meaning but applied to a body of water, to glass, or to some other transparent substance.

## 8. macabre

A grotesque situation or condition is incongruous, unnatural, or even shocking, but not gruesome or death-haunted. It may be fantastic, bizarre, eccentric, or absurd but is more likely to be ludicrous than grim. A Halloween skeleton costume is grotesque, but a real skeleton found under the house would be gruesome.

## 9. mature

The Latin root is *maturus,* ripe. Synonyms include *developed, ripened,* and *aged.* (Also point up *mature* as a verb, with its synonyms.)

## 10. nebulous

*Indistinct* has a similar meaning but different uses. *Obscure, enigmatic,* and *cryptic* are stronger words implying deliberate unclearness. *Lucid, distinct, obvious* are antonyms.

## 11. pensive

The Middle French root of *reverie* means to wander or be delirious. *Ruminate* (WW p. 12), meaning to muse or meditate, is also defined as to chew the cud.

## 12. placid

Synonyms of *placidity* include *quietude, tranquillity,* and *serenity.*

## 13. plaintive

Compare *nostalgic* (WW p. 222), which is not a synonym and yet nostalgia usually invokes plaintiveness.

## 14. plausible

A work of fiction is *plausible* if it appears true or reasonable. It is *credible* if it is believable. Thus, the story of a man who escaped from prison in a garbage can is *plausible* but hardly *credible* because it has rarely if ever been done.

## 15. potent

–Pot– words include, in addition to potential, *potentiality, potentate, impotent,* and *impotence. Potable, potion, potation* come from the Latin infinitive *potare,* to drink.

16. **pungent**

   *Expunge* and *puncture* come from the same Latin verb, *pungere,* to prick.

17. **rigorous**

   *Strictness* is exact and undeviating. *Rigidity* is stiff, unyielding, and inflexible. *Rigor(ousness)* is strict and exacting to the point of being burdensome or causing hardship. Antonyms include *lax* and *flexible*.

18. **wanton**

   The word is of Old English origin. It may mean frisky or playful when applied to a child or a natural force that is unpredictable and not very destructive. It may also mean lavish or luxuriant when applied to vegetation. Sometimes the word is used as a noun, especially for a morally irresponsible person, or as a verb meaning to waste one's time in luxurious pastimes.

19. **wary**

   *Aware* and *beware* are from the same Old English root. Antonyms include *incautious, unsuspecting, rash*.

20. **wily**

   *Wiles* are tricks, artifices, stratagems, especially of enemies and of dishonest persons. The word is of Old English origin.

# KEYS

**First Practice Set**

| | |
|---|---|
| *First Para:* | obese, placid |
| | pensive, brusque |
| | candid, nebulous |
| | lucid, wary |
| | furtive |
| *Second Para:* | wanton |
| | dour, plausible |
| | delinquent, macabre |
| *Third Para:* | rigorous |
| | plaintive, pungent |
| | potent, wily |
| | mature |

**Second Practice Set**

1. demure, bovine
2. stringent, rigid
3. caustic, glib
4. coherent, grisly
5. wistful, reverie
6. piquant, impudent
7. stoical, surly
8. aromatic, weird
9. chary, credible
10. blatant, imperturbable

40/part one

**Third Practice Set**

**A.**

| | | | |
|---|---|---|---|
| 1. | 5 | 6. | 1 |
| 2. | 9 | 7. | 12 |
| 3. | 7 | 8. | 2 |
| 4. | 10 | 9. | 4 |
| 5. | 8 | 10. | 6 |

**B.**

| | | | |
|---|---|---|---|
| 1. | 5 | 6. | 9 |
| 2. | 8 | 7. | 1 |
| 3. | 4 | 8. | 3 |
| 4. | 10 | 9. | 12 |
| 5. | 7 | 10. | 6 |

## UNIT TEST  *(Word Wealth Testing Program)*

1. m (brusque);  s (candor)
2. p (caustic);  g (dour)
3. c (delinquent);  u (placidity)
4. bb (nebulousness);  z (maturity)
5. f (surly);  a (imperturbable)
6. cc (pensiveness);  y (wariness)
7. v (plaintiff);  l (gruesome)
8. q (weird);  h (macabre)
9. x (lucidity);  t (plausibility)
10. i (obese);  e (coherent)
11. o (bovine);  r (surreptitious)
12. b (austere);  j (tranquil);  n (wily)

# unit four

## CHOICES

1. b (cleanse)
2. d (outcast)
3. c (refer to as example)
4. b (satisfy to excess)
5. c (spread through)
6. a (messenger)
7. d (descriptive title)
8. a (opening)
9. d (brief story)
10. b (take offense at)

## VERBS

1. **abate**

   *Dwindle* is a synonym that goes well with the poetic "ebb" words. Note that *decrease, diminish,* and *lessen,* unlike the "ebb" words, may be used transitively.

2. **cite**

   This word comes from the Latin *citare,* to summon or arouse, and has two homonyms in English, *sight* and *site.*

3. **entice**

   The word has unsuspected fire in its roots, which appears in both the French verb *enticier,* to set afire, and the Latin root *titio,* a burning brand. A *decoy* (a person or device used to lure a victim into danger) is an additional mode of inducement.

4. **frustrate**

   *Baffle,* a near synonym, usually falls short of *frustrate.* Compare *stymie,* a situation in golf in which an opponent's ball lies in the line between a player's ball and the hole. Hence the verb meaning of *stymie,* to block.

5. **manifest**

   The root meaning of striking or seizing (Latin, *fendere*) the hand (*manus*) suggests the dramatic way in which one brings another person's attention to something that is arresting. Other –manu– (hand) words (WW p. 343) may be mentioned, such as *maniple, manipulate, manual, manufacture, manumission,* and *manuscript.*

6. **pervade**

Note that *invade* and its variants also come from the Latin verb *vadere*, to go.

7. **purge**

This is a good word to study for levels of meaning, from the literal use of fires and chemicals as purging agents to the metaphoric and intellectual-spiritual uses. The word comes from the Latin verb *purgare*, to cleanse, and this in turn has been traced to the adjective *purus*, pure, combined with *agere*, to do or act.

8. **reproach**

*Reproachless* may be added: "The monk lived a *reproachless* life." Note that *approach* and its variants come from the same Latin root, *prope*, near.

9. **resent**

*Consent, assent, sentiment, presentiment, sentient, sentience,* and their variant forms all come from the Latin verb *sentire*, to feel (see –sent– WW p. 342). However, *absent* and *present* come from *esse*, to be.

10. **satiate**

*Satisfy, dissatisfied, unsatisfied,* and their variants come from the same root as *satiate*, which is Latin *satis*, enough. Even the word *sad* is traced to this root by *Webster's New World Dictionary;* but *Webster's New Collegiate Dictionary* traces it to the Old English word *saed*, satisfied, akin to *satis*.

## NOUNS

1. **abyss**

Compare *chasm, crevasse, gorge*. A *chasm* is a deep crevice or crack in the earth's surface. A *crevasse* is also a fissure, usually in a glacier, and a *gorge* is a chasm if the opening is rather narrow.

2. **anecdote**

The Greek root means not published, from *an*, not, plus *ek*, out, plus a form of *didomai*, give. An *anecdote* is thus literally something not given out. *Anecdotist* is sometimes used to refer to habitual storytellers. (*Antidote* [WW p. 295] is a remedy to counter the effect of a poison.)

3. **aperture**

In discussing cameras and telescopes, the word denotes the diameter of the opening. A student might explain the standard camera designations *f* 3.5, *f* 4.5, etc.

4. derelict

   The Latin root is *linquere*, leave, with two prefixes, de– and re–, which have an intensive effect. It is the root of *relinquish* and *delinquent*.

5. epithet

   "The merry monarch" or "a good soul" are other examples of adjectival epithets. A pupil may compile a list of ten epithets from history, like "Richard the Lion-Hearted" or the "Roughriders"; from fiction, like "Lord Jim"; from local school life; or from community affairs.

6. fiend

   The word is of Old English derivation, Anglo-Saxon *feond* being one of its ancient forms. It is a good word for a thesaurus exercise. The Arch Fiend is the Devil or Satan.

7. harbinger
   One of its ancestors is *herberge*, in Old French a word for shelter.

8. lament

   This word is applied chiefly to situations, actions, or ideas rather than persons. Perhaps it is for this reason that *lamentable* evokes less feeling than *painful*, *lugubrious*, or *deplorable*.

9. omen

   Note that *ominous* is the adjective form. *Augury* is an additional synonym.

10. pestilence

    The Latin root is *pestis*, plague, from which the word *pest* also comes. Like *derelict*, the word lends itself especially well to metaphoric and symbolic use, as in *The Plague* by Albert Camus (*La Peste* in French).

# KEYS

Word Forays

1. present (*p* added to *resent*)
2. incite (by rearranging the letters of entry word *entice* and changing the first letter)
3. –vade– means to go.

## First Practice Set

1. abyss, abate
2. enticed, omen
3. anecdotes, frustrate
4. fiend, manifest
5. pestilence, lament
6. cite, resent
7. pervaded, satiate
8. derelict, purge
9. epithet, reproach
10. aperture, harbinger

## Second Practice Set

1. waxes, wanes
2. reprimand, appellation
3. rueful, incite
4. chide, dotage
5. fissure, presentiment
6. lure, beguile
7. sate, glut
8. cajole, upbraid
9. precursor, diminish
10. circumvent, permeate

## Third Practice Set

**A.**
1. 7
2. 6
3. 8
4. 9
5. 10
6. 11
7. 3
8. 5
9. 12
10. 2

**B.**
1. 7
2. 6
3. 1
4. 12
5. 5
6. 10
7. 3
8. 11
9. 8
10. 2

## UNIT TEST  *(Word Wealth Testing Program)*

1. cc (frustrate);  b (derelict)
2. n (anecdote);  v (entice)
3. r (diminish);  y (pervade);  h (pestilence)
4. s (abate);  e (satiety)
5. f (aperture);  k (abyss)
6. bb (resent);  j (surfeit)
7. p (reproach);  u (upbraid)
8. w (reprimand);  a (fiend)
9. c (purgative);  z (subside)
10. i (omen);  l (precursor)
11. aa (manifest);  o (inveigle)
12. q (lament);  g (epithet)

# unit five

## PLUS

1. a (adhere)   2. b (chastise)   3. c (extricate)   4. c (conjecture)
5. c (elation)   6. d (dexterity)   7. b (emulate)   8. a (avarice)
9. c (apathy)   10. d (diverge)

## VERBS

1. **adhere**

   The sentences illustrate two levels of usage, literal and abstract-metaphorical. See also –ad– (WW p. 277) and –here–, –hes– (WW p. 280).

2. **alter**

   *Alterant* (anything which causes alteration) may be added to the list. Also *alterative* (causing change or that which causes change), *alterably, unalterable,* and *unalterably*. Like *alter*, the word *alternate* and its variant forms come from the Latin *alter*, other. *Altar* (a place for sacrifices) comes from the Latin *altus*, high.

3. **assail**

   This word comes from the Latin word *ad*, against, and *salire*, to leap. *Beset* and *bombard* may be added to the list of synonyms. *Besiege* is a more passive and less violent way to attack a city or a person.

4. **augment**

   *Exacerbation* is the sharpening or worsening of an annoyance, disease, or tension. *Burgeoning* is a sprouting, budding, or rapid growth.

5. **chastise**

   *Chasten* (to purify by suffering, hardship, or punishment); and *chaste* (pure and virtuous) come more directly from the same Latin root as *chastise*. The root is *castus*, pure. Thus *chastise* implies the idea of making a person more virtuous by punishment and not merely rendering justice for its own sake.

## 6. disperse

The root –sperse– is presented on p. 332 of *Word Wealth*.

## 7. diverge

Like *disperse, diverge* is used in both a literal and figurative sense with regard to paths, routes, persons, or ideas.

## 8. emulate

*Emulous,* eager to equal or surpass, and *emulator* are used occasionally.

## 9. extricate

The adverb form, *inextricably,* is often used: "Because the two students are roommates, their clothes, their lives, and their affairs have become *inextricably* entangled." Compare *intricate.*

## 10. forage

The root is a series of French words for fodder, but the word has come to denote the act of seeking food or other necessities aggressively.

# NOUNS

## 1. antagonist

*Protagonist* and other terms from Greek drama are presented on p. 269 of *Word Wealth,* along with the root *agon,* struggle, from which the word *agony* comes.

## 2. apathy

*Nonchalance* (WW p. 248), an attitude of indifference or unconcern, may be a result of apathy but is not necessarily a synonym.

## 3. avarice

Add *cupidity* (greed, excessive desire for wealth), cited on pp. 143 and 249 of *Word Wealth:* "The bandit's *cupidity* made him a criminal and finally cost him his life." The word comes from the Latin word *cupere,* to desire strongly, which is also the root of *Cupid.*

## 4. clarity

From the Latin root *clarus,* clear, come also *Clara, clarabella* (velvety organ tone), *Clare, Clarence, claret, Claribel, Clarissa,* and *declare.*

5. **conjecture**

   The –ject– words are presented on p. 288 of *Word Wealth*.

6. **defiance**

   *Defiance* is more active and more likely to be verbal than are *opposition* and *antagonism*, both of which are normally passive states of tension. *Antagonism* is more active than *opposition*, however. To *contravene* a person's rights is to oppose or deny them actively.

7. **dexterity**

   The word comes from the Latin word *dexter*, right (hand). The element –dexter– is treated on p. 312 of *Word Wealth*.

8. **discretion**

   *Discretionary* powers of an executive are those which he may use as his judgment dictates. The negative forms are *indiscreet* and *indiscretion*.

9. **exertion**

   *Desert, insert,* and *assert* come from the same Latin root, *serere,* to join; but *inert* has an altogether different derivation.

10. **exuberance**

    The verb form, *exuberate,* is sometimes used: "Sparrows *exuberate* noisily in the backyard."

# KEYS

**First Practice Set**

1. adhere, forage
2. clarity, diverge
3. conjecture, alter
4. antagonist, assail
5. exuberance, apathy
6. chastise, exertion
7. extricate, disperse
8. emulate, dexterity
9. discretion
10. avarice, augment, defiance

**Second Practice Set**

1. enhance, elation
2. prudence, covetous
3. circumspection, lethargy
4. transport, transfigure
5. intensification, aggravation
6. diversify, accretion
7. assault, ebullience
8. torpor, proficiency
9. alter ego, endeavor
10. transmute, ravaged

## Third Practice Set

A.

1. 5
2. 10
3. 8
4. 11
5. 6
6. 12
7. 9
8. 4
9. 1
10. 2

B.

1. 11
2. 9
3. 4
4. 1
5. 6
6. 2
7. 3
8. 5
9. 12
10. 8

## Unit Test    (*Word Wealth Testing Program*)

1. n (adherence);  w (disperse)
2. y (assail);  b (avarice)
3. v (clarify);  q (augment)
4. cc (diversify);  k (increment)
5. h (aggravation);  z (alter);
   o (defiance)
6. m (assumption);  e (exertion)
7. c (antagonist);  g (hypothesis)
8. l (speculation);  j (proficiency)
9. bb (transfigure);  a (elation)
10. f (prudence);  x (extricate)
11. i (apathy);  t (emulate)
12. w (diverge);  aa (ravage)

# unit six

## QUIBBLES

1. b (a firefly)
2. a (spiteful)
3. d (a hot afternoon)
4. a (lavish)
5. d (harmful)
6. b (in a trailer)
7. d (practiced at night)
8. a (plentiful)
9. c (outstanding)
10. a (merciful)

## ADJECTIVES

1. **copious**

   The Latin root is *ops*, wealth, from which *opulence* (WW p. 106) also comes. Compare *cornucopia*, horn of plenty, in Greek mythology.

2. **eminent**

   *Prominent* and *preeminent*, which come from the same Latin root *minēre*, to project, are close to *eminent* in meaning as applied to persons and objects. Unlike *prominence*, however, *eminence* is more often used in the literal sense of the third illustrative sentence. The form *eminency* is used very little.

3. **frugal**

   *Prodigality, prodigious,* and *prodigy* are good antonymic words indicating enormousness or quantitative excess. The root of *prodigal* is *agere*, to act or drive; the root of the *prodigy* group is *aio*, I say.

4. **languid**

   *Listlessness* is languor, but *languor* is pleasanter. *Apathy* (no feeling) is more an intellectual than a merely physical kind of unconcern.

5. **hostile**

   *Host* (an army, multitude, or large number) comes from the same root, *hostis*, enemy; but *host* (one who entertains) along with *hospitable, hostel, hotel, hospitality, hospital,* comes from the Latin noun *hospes*, guest. The root may be traced back to *hostis*, however, and the link lies in the use of *hostis* as foreigner or stranger, who may be either a guest or an enemy—or both.

6. **laudable**

   "Laus Deo," meaning "Praise (be) to God," is a Latin phrase containing the root of *laudable*. *Applaud*, however, is from *plaudere*, to clap hands.

7. **lenient**

   *Lenience, lenitive,* and *lenity* are less familiar forms.

8. **luminous**

   *Lumen* is a unit by which to measure the intensity of a light or a light source. *Illuminate* and *illumine* are verb forms.

9. **nocturnal**

   *Noct–*, night, appears in *noctambulism* (sleepwalking) also in the names of various night creatures such as *noctule* (a kind of brown bat) and *noctuid* moths.

10. **oblique**

    In military usage it is used to indicate a turn of approximately 45°. For this purpose the word is pronounced *ō-blīké*.

11. **obnoxious**

    *Innocent, innocuous,* and *nocent* (causing harm) also come from the Latin verb *nocere*, to harm.

12. **obtrusive**

    *Unobtrusive(ly)* is probably the most familiar form of the word. Compare *intrude, intrusive* (to thrust oneself into someone's affairs or privacy in an unwelcome manner).

13. **perpetual**

    Note that *continuous* implies uninterrupted continuance, whereas a *continual* occurrence may actually be intermittent. *Imperishable* and *everlasting* are more poetic and more hyperbolic than *perpetual*.

14. **regal**

    *Regent, regency, regicide, regime, regimen, region, regiment,* and *regular* are all traceable to the same root, *regere*, to rule.

15. **vagrant**

    *Vague* and *vagary* also come from the Latin *vagus*, to wander.

16. **vehement**

    The root *vehere*, to carry, is also the root of *vehicle* and *vehicular*.

17. **vindictive**

    Several related words are listed under *rancor* (WW p. 163). *Reprisal* is presented on p. 107 of *Word Wealth*.

18. **vociferous**

    Some other words from the Latin –vox–, –voci–, voice, include *vocal, vociferate, voice, vox angelica, vox humana, vox populi*. The three *vox* words are all foreign phrases that have not been "naturalized" in American usage and must therefore be italicized in written work. Compare *equivocal*.

19. **vulnerable**

    The Latin root *vulnerare* means to wound. Thus the literal meaning is able to be wounded. Antonym: *invulnerable*.

20. **zealous**

    *Zealous* rhymes with *jealous*.

# KEYS

**First Practice Set**

1. vociferous, vehement
2. obtrusive, obnoxious
3. perpetual, luminous
4. vagrant, nocturnal
5. vindictive, copious
6. vulnerable, languid
7. hostile, zealous
8. lenient, laudable
9. eminent, frugal
10. regal, oblique

**Second Practice Set**

1. fanatic, luminescent
2. prodigal, languish
3. nocturne, renowned
4. vagabond, devious
5. profuse, obstreperous
6. interminable, noxious
7. marathon, notorious
8. itinerants, adverse
9. incessant, odious
10. averse (to), bigots
11. boisterous, apathetic
12. lassitude, celebrated

**Third Practice Set**

A.

| | | | |
|---|---|---|---|
| 1. | 6 | 6. | 11 |
| 2. | 10 | 7. | 12 |
| 3. | 4 | 8. | 8 |
| 4. | 2 | 9. | 3 |
| 5. | 1 | 10. | 5 |

B.

| | | | |
|---|---|---|---|
| 1. | 11 | 6. | 8 |
| 2. | 6 | 7. | 4 |
| 3. | 1 | 8. | 5 |
| 4. | 9 | 9. | 2 |
| 5. | 12 | 10. | 3 |

## Unit Test     (*Word Wealth Testing Program*)

1. cc (frugality);   d (laudable)
2. e (eminent);   x (hostility)
3. j (renowned);   i (regal)
4. g (vehement);   m (celebrated)
5. b (profuse);   s (obtrusiveness);   ee (vociferousness)
6. k (boisterous);   h (nocturnal)
7. u (fanatics);   n (vulnerable)
8. r (obnoxiousness);   o (odious)
9. w (officiousness);   dd (vindictiveness)
10. n (vagabond);   a (bigoted)
11. v (lassitude);   y (aversion)
12. aa (leniency);   f (luminous)

# unit seven

## WHICH WORD?

1. c (repose)
2. a (tyranny)
3. d (succor)
4. c (indignant)
5. b (sanction)
6. c (inane)
7. b (strategy)
8. a (implicit)
9. b (exultant)
10. a (inert)

## ADJECTIVES

1. **acute**

    The Latin root, *acuere,* to sharpen, is the word from which come *acuity, acumen,* and *acuminate* (tapering to a point).

2. **agile**

    *Supple* comes from the Latin *supplex,* suppliant. *Lithe* may also be introduced: A lithe figure, a ballet dancer's for example, is pliant, limber, easily bent.

3. **erratic**

    Compare *inerrant,* never deviating from truth, never wrong.

4. **exorbitant**

    It comes from Latin *orbita,* a track or orbit, and is closely related to *orb, orbicular,* and *orbit,* which come from *orbis,* a circle.

5. **exultant**

    *Exultant* comes from the Latin *saltare,* to leap, whereas *exalt* is traced to *altus,* high. *Assault* is derived from *salire,* to leap, as is *assail* (WW p. 35).

6. **implicit**

    Note that it is one of the –plic– words from *plicare,* to fold (WW p. 340).

7. **inane**

    The Latin root is *inanis,* empty.

8. **inert**

   From *ars, artis*, skill or art, it implies lack of skill rather than of activity.

9. **inferior**

   *Infernal* comes from the same Latin root, *inferus*, below.

10. **infernal**

    Additions to the list of "hell" words may include: *Hades* (Greek underworld), *Sheol* (Hebrew equivalent), Inferno (Dante's), and the *nether regions* (below or underneath).

# NOUNS

1. **fugitive**

   From the same root, *fugere*, to flee, come *refuge, refugee, centrifugal, centrifuge, fugacious* (fleeting, lasting but a short time), and *fugue* (a musical composition).

2. **indignation**

   *Dignity* comes from the same root, meaning worthy or to be worthy.

3. **insolence**

   *Impertinent* may be added to the list under *brusque* (WW p. 18). *Impertinence* is disrespectfulness that goes beyond the bounds of propriety but is less offensive than *insolence* or *impudence* (shamelessness).

4. **obeisance**

   It comes from the French word *obeir*, to obey.

5. **repose**

   Compare *compose, depose, dispose, discompose, expose, impose, oppose, pose, propose, suppose*, and their variant forms. The total list from the two interwoven and almost inextricable roots is one of the longest lists derivable from a pair of Latin roots.

6. **retinue**

   It is a derivative, via French, of the Latin *tenere*, to hold, and thus one of the dozens of –tain–, –ten(t) words in English (see WW p. 298).

7. **sanction**

   Literally it means made holy, from the Latin *sanctus,* holy. For other –sanct– words see WW p. 362. *Connivance* is another kind of approval that may be included in the study of *sanction.*

8. **strategy**

   The word comes from the Greek word *stratēgos,* a general, which in turn comes from two Greek words meaning to lead an army. It is more inclusive than words like *artifice, ruse, wile,* or *maneuver.*

9. **succor**

   This word is one of the less obvious derivatives of *currere,* to run (see –cur(r)–, –curs–, –course–, WW p. 304).

10. **tyranny**

    Like *strategy,* it is a word of Greek ancestry, coming from *tyrannos,* ruler with absolute power, usurper. The verb form is *tyrannize.* Mankind has found considerable use for *tyrannicide,* the act of killing a tyrant or the person who kills him.

# KEYS

**First Practice Set**

1. fugitive, erratic
2. acute, inferior
3. indignation, succor
4. exultant, insolence
5. infernal, repose
6. agile, obeisance
7. inane, retinue
8. tyranny, exorbitant
9. strategy, inert
10. implicit, sanction

**Second Practice Set**

1. jubilation, vexation
2. cortège, resentment
3. indolent, passive
4. nimble, salaam
5. aberration, despot
6. inordinate, autocrat
7. animosity, indulgence
8. dispensation, jubilee
9. execrable, immoderate
10. diabolic(al), listless

**Third Practice Set**

A.
1. 7
2. 10
3. 6
4. 1
5. 11
6. 2
7. 12
8. 3
9. 4
10. 8

B.
1. 3
2. 8
3. 6
4. 7
5. 12
6. 1
7. 9
8. 10
9. 4
10. 2

## Unit Test   (Word Wealth Testing Program)

1. f (inane); bb (acuteness)
2. q (insolence); x (indignation)
3. r (exasperation); j (erratic)
4. cc (obeisance); w (genuflection)
5. n (jubilation); l (strategy)
6. a (diabolic); t (tyrant)
7. i (indolent); h (inferior)
8. e (erroneous); m (tactics)
9. b (implicit); u (aberration)
10. aa (vexation); y (agility)
11. d (dormant); p (repose)
12. v (succor); z (sanction); k (despot)

# unit eight

## ARMY NOTES

1. b (martial)  2. a (valiant)  3. d (subjugate)  4. b (surmount)
5. c (negligent)  6. c (traverse)  7. d (servile)  8. c (remonstrate)
9. a (precarious)  10. a (redundant)

## VERBS

1. **impute**

   *Impute* is the verb of a family of words from the Latin *putare,* to estimate, calculate, or think. The class may list *compute, depute* (give authority), *dispute, repute,* and their variant forms. Several are listed under –pute–, –putat– (WW p. 340).

2. **renounce**

   *Renounce* is one of the –nounce–, –nunci–, declare, words (see WW p. 306).

3. **reprimand**

   The root is *reprimere,* to repress. Other –press– words, from *primere* or its derivative *pressare,* include *express, depress, impress, repress, suppress,* and their variants.

4. **requite**

   This word derives from the adjective *quit,* free or rid of. *Compensate* is an additional related word.

5. **segregate**

   See –greg–, gather in a group, (WW p. 316).

6. **subjugate**

   The root –junc(t)–, –juga–, join, (WW p. 307) appears in a number of English words.

#### 7. surmount

*Transcend*, with much the same meaning (to climb over or across), is less likely to be used on the literal or physical level. List other *mount* words like *dismount, remount, mountain,* etc.

#### 8. tabulate

*Compile* is a related word of broader meaning. A *tabulator* is a device on a typewriter to speed up the typing of material in columns.

#### 9. traverse

The prefix trans– (WW p. 278) and the root –vert–, –vers– (WW p. 299) make the word easy to remember.

#### 10. vilify

From the root, *vilis*, base or evil, come *vile* and *revile*. *Villain*, however, comes from *villanus*, a farm servant, and *villa*, a country home.

# ADJECTIVES

#### 1. intricate

*Intrigue*, plotting, which is usually intricate, comes from the same Latin root *tricae*, perplexities, impediments. Compare *extricate* (WW p. 36).

#### 2. martial

The word *warlike* implies an eagerness to fight. *Military* connotes discipline and a certain rigor, though it is applied to any kind of equipment or activity related to armed forces. *Martial* suggests the pomp and the parade spirit of warfare more than it does the equipment, the discipline, or the fighting.

#### 3. negligible

*Negligible* shares the root –neg–, not, with *neglect, negation, negligee,* and their variant forms. *Negligence* and *negligibility* might also be included.

#### 4. obstinate

Six forms of wrong-headed tenacity may be mentioned: *bigotry* (blind, intolerant devotion), *monomania* (state of being carried away and irrational on a single topic), *obsession* (WW p. 12), *intolerance, infatuation* (unreasonable attachment) (WW p. 220), and *zealotry* (excessive devotion to a cause) (WW p. 48).

## 5. precarious

From the same root (*precari*, to ask earnestly) as *pray* and *prayer*, it suggests the unreliability implicit in the phrase "on a wing and a prayer." Compare *imprecation* (WW p. 133).

## 6. redundant

*Redundant* is actually an adjective form of *redound*, to react, result, or recoil; it has an almost onomatopoetic quality, like the two Latin roots from which the word comes: *undare*, to surge or swell, and *unda*, wave. Also from the root comes the word *undulate* (WW p. 152).

## 7. requisite

*Perquisite* is formed on the same root, *quaerere*, to seek (see –quir–, –quisit–, WW p. 306 under –rog–).

## 8. servile

This is a good place to mention other adjectives ending in –ile, such as *fragile*, *juvenile*, *puerile* (WW p. 143), and *senile* (WW p. 91).

## 9. sundry

The word family in this case is a small one, from Old English.

## 10. valiant

*Valid, value,* and *validate* are a few of the words which can also be traced to the Latin verb *valere,* to be strong.

# KEYS

**First Practice Set**

1. redundant, servile
2. intricate, surmount
3. valiant, martial
4. reprimanded, imputed
5. segregate, obstinate
6. subjugate, negligible
7. vilify, precarious
8. requisite, requite
9. renounce, traverse
10. tabulate, sundry

**Second Practice Set**

1. inflexible, waive
2. rectify, restitution
3. remonstrance, vituperative
4. obduracy, subservient
5. pertinacity, censure
6. abdicate, forgo
7. berate, negligent
8. intrepid, tenacity
9. revile, obsequious
10. vanquish, quell

## Third Practice Set

**A.**

| | | | |
|---|---|---|---|
| 1. 5 | | 6. 12 | |
| 2. 9 | | 7. 4 | |
| 3. 7 | | 8. 6 | |
| 4. 1 | | 9. 3 | |
| 5. 10 | | 10. 8 | |

**B.**

| | | | |
|---|---|---|---|
| 1. 4 | | 6. 2 | |
| 2. 9 | | 7. 6 | |
| 3. 12 | | 8. 3 | |
| 4. 5 | | 9. 7 | |
| 5. 11 | | 10. 8 | |

## Changes and Charges

1. impu*t*e/impu*r*e; requi*t*e/requi*r*e; *m*artial/*p*artial.

2. Other words ending in *–nounce: announce, denounce, pronounce;* in *–mand: countermand, remand* (the *–mand* here, however, comes from Latin *mandare,* to give in one's hand, not, as in *reprimand,* from *primere,* to press or check); in *–verse: adverse, averse, perverse, reverse, verse;* in *–ile* (in addition to those mentioned here on p. 59): *percentile, prehensile*.

## Unit Test  *(Word Wealth Testing Program)*

1. y (subjugate); o (tenacity)
2. z (waive); b (negligible)
3. dd (relinquish); u (reparation)
4. n (perseverance);
   bb (renounce)
5. k (reprimand);
   m (doggedness)
6. ee (vanquish); x (vilify);
   t (vituperation)
7. e (martial); j (valiant)
8. w (inflexibility);
   c (precarious)
9. d (negligent); i (intricate)
10. p (censure); s (reproof)
11. h (redundant);
    l (remonstrance)
12. f (subservient); q (obduracy)

# unit nine

## EXAMPLES

1. initiative
2. anomaly
3. hypothesis
4. perquisite
5. enervation
6. complement
7. nadir
8. exaltation
9. apogee
10. consolation
11. arson
12. apocalypse
13. mosaic
14. litany
15. maxim

## NOUNS

1. **anomaly**

    A Greek-derived word from a–, not, plus *homos,* the same. *Homos* is one of the roots of *homonym, homogenous,* and other homo– words (WW p. 352).

2. **apogee**

    It combines the Greek prefix apo– (from) with the Greek word for earth, *ge.*

3. **apocalypse**

    From the Greek root *kalyptein,* to cover, and apo–, with the sense of from, we get the meaning to uncover, *i.e.,* to reveal. The "Four Horsemen of the Apocalypse" are thought to represent Conquest, War, Famine, and Death.

4. **arson**

    A good place to bring in *pyromaniac* (firebug), *pyromancy* (fortune-telling by interpretation of flames), *pyrophobia* (abnormal fear of fire), and other fire words. An average college-sized dictionary lists sixty words beginning with pyro–, most of them technical or scientific terms. Fire words from the Latin root flam– include *flambeau* (lighted torch), *flamboyant* (showy, bombastic, flaming), *flamingo* (a red bird), *flammable* (now replacing *inflammable* because the meaning is clearer).

5. **client**

    The root clinare, to lean, links *client* and *clientele* with the word cluster that contains *incline, decline, recline, disinclined.*

## 6. hypothesis

Other hypo– (beneath, below), words include *hypocrite*, *hypodermic* (under the skin), *hypostasis* (settling of the blood in the lower parts of the body).

## 7. incidence

Note that it is one of the –cide– (cut or kill) words (WW p. 332). Others are *decide, suicide, coincidence,* and their variant forms.

## 8. initiative

*Initiate, initial,* and *initiatory* may be cited additionally.

## 9. litany

The metaphorical meaning of this word makes it applicable even to the sounds of machinery or the hum of insects. See WW, pp. xiv (3.) and 70.

## 10. maxim

*Maximize*, to intensify or heighten as much as possible, is the verb form. A *saw* is a homespun or folksy saying that is open to question, like "Beggars can't be choosers." *Axiom, theorem,* and *postulate* (WW p. 38) may well be reviewed or introduced at this point, though they belong primarily to mathematics. An *axiom* is a generally accepted principle that, by its very nature, cannot be proved: "Bad money drives out good money." A *theorem* or *thesis* (WW pp. 38, 237) is a proposition to be demonstrated: "The sum of the internal angles of a triangle is always 180°." A *postulate* is something that is assumed to be true and is taken as a premise: "A straight line is the shortest distance between two points."

## 11. mosaic

This word goes back to the Greek word *Mousa*, Muse. A *mosaicist* designs, produces, or sells mosaics. But the *Mosaic* law is so called because it is ascribed to Moses (from the Hebrew *Mōsheh*).

## 12. perquisite

A *gratuity* or tip is a *perquisite* given in return for services rendered by waiters and others.

# VERBS

## 1. complement

This verb is derived from the Latin verb, *plere, pletus,* fill, which also gives us the word *complete.* Compare the plen– words from *plenus,* full: *plenary, plenty,* etc. (WW p. 316) The reason for the spelling of *complement* may be stressed, with *compliment* juxtaposed.

2. **console**

    The Latin root is *solari,* to solace or comfort. *Console* as applied to a wall bracket, to a desklike frame for organ controls, or to a television cabinet that stands on the floor, illustrates the way a word can diverge from its basic meaning.

3. **consummate**

    The root is the Latin *summa,* highest, as in *summa cum laude,* the highest (honors) with praise. It is not related to *consume, consumption* or other words of one *m* from *sumere, sumptus,* take.

4. **enervate**

    The literal meaning, to take the "nerve" or spirit out of (e–) a person, helps one remember it.

5. **exalt**

    The literal Latin meaning is to move out or up (ex–) high (altus). Compare *altitude, altimeter, altar* (but NOT *alter*).

6. **perforate**

    Per– (through) is combined with *forare,* to bore (holes).

7. **propagate**

    The basic Latin meaning is a slip for transplanting, with the implication of taking root and growing.

8. **stipulate**

    The root meaning of the word is to bargain. As the spelling indicates, no connection with *stipend* or *stipple* exists.

# KEYS

## First Practice Set

1. stipulates, arson
2. mosaic, anomaly
3. initiative, clients
4. console, hypothesis
5. litany, apogee
6. incidence, enervate
7. apocalypse, maxim
8. perquisites, exalt
9. consummate, propagate
10. perforate, complement

## Second Practice Set

1. clientele, consummate
2. dictum, canon
3. proverb, truism
4. adage, stipulate
5. epigram
6. maxim, aphorism
7. theorem, axiom
8. perigee, zenith, exaltation
9. bounty
10. initiator, bonus

## Third Practice Set

**A.**
1. 6
2. 4
3. 10
4. 1
5. 9
6. 12
7. 5
8. 11
9. 8
10. 2

**B.**
1. 3
2. 10
3. 8
4. 12
5. 1
6. 5
7. 4
8. 7
9. 6
10. 9

## Unit Test  *(Word Wealth Testing Program)*

1. j (apocalypse); b (anomalous)
2. g (arson); r (initiative)
3. n (liturgy); y (complement)
4. w (stipulate); q (perquisite)
5. a (aphoristic); e (epigrammatic)
6. p (canon); i (maxim)
7. k (dividend); h (hypothesis)
8. c (exalted); s (zenith); l (fulfillment)
9. aa (console); x (sabotage)
10. f (incendiary); d (enervating)
11. u (propagate); t (mosaic)
12. z (atrophy); v (perforate)

# unit ten

## THEY CREATED WORDS

1. wealthy power figure
2. living chiefly for sensual pleasure
3. intellectual-aesthetic
4. extended journey
5. powerful, gigantic
6. airtight or magical
7. too costly
8. something that insures safety
9. daring on behalf of humanity
10. dancing
11. taking ruthless action to attain conformity

## NOUNS

1. **aegis**

   A Latin word from a similar Greek word for the goatskin shield of Zeus, *aegis* is traceable to the Greek word for goat.

2. **amazon**

   The Amazon River in Brazil was so named by Spaniards who believed that female warriors lived on its shores. The word literally means without (a–) breast (*mazos*) because the original Amazons were supposed to have cut off one of their breasts for greater skill in archery.

3. **aurora**

   *Eos* was the name of the Greek goddess of dawn. From it comes the prefix eo– in *eohippus* (early horse), *Eolithic* (early part of Stone Age), and *eosin* (a dawn-colored dye).

4. **odyssey**

   If time permits, list other words from famous names, such as the Earl of Sandwich, Stentor, Mentor, Jeremiah, Dr. J. I. Guillotine, Mausolus, Nimrod, Solon, Captain Charles Boycott, Charles Lynch, F. A. Mesmer, etc.

5. **paean**

   Carried over into Latin, the word means hymn.

## 6. palladium

Palladium is also a rare metal of the platinum group used in alloys and in other ways.

## 7. plutocrat

*Plutus* was the blind Greek god of wealth, and *plutocrat* comes from his Greek name *Ploutos*. *Pluto,* the Greek god of the ancient underworld or Hades, is today the name of the outermost or ninth planet of our solar system. (**Note:** If the celestial body recently discovered between Saturn and Uranus is identified as a planet, Pluto would then, of course, be designated the tenth planet of our solar system.)

## 8. siren

Today a group of vegetarian sea mammals takes its name from the same Greek root.

## 9. Valhalla

The *Valkyries* were maidens of Odin (the supreme deity of Norse myth) who conducted the souls of heroes slain in battle to Valhalla and waited on them there.

# ADJECTIVES

## 1. ambrosial

The *Ambrosian* type of liturgical chant, introduced by St. Ambrose, was a more ornamental form than the plain Gregorian chant that later replaced it.

## 2. Apollonian

It was German philosopher Nietzsche who described this life style and applied the terms Apollonian and Dionysian to the dual impulses.

## 3. Dionysian

Thomas Mann's *Death in Venice* is the story of a writer who, escaping from an excess of the Apollonian life, permitted the Dionysian mode to overcome and destroy him.

## 4. hermetic

*Hermes* was also the god of science, of commerce, and of oratory, with a reputation for cunning. He conducted the spirits of dead persons to Hades.

5. **Procrustean**

   This myth emphasizes the absurdity or pointless cruelty of insisting on strict conformity in matters where variety and individuality are in no way objectionable.

6. **Promethean**

   Prometheus has had a strong romantic, if not revolutionary, following over the centuries for a varied assortment of enthusiasts, from poets like Shelley to nuclear scientists of the twentieth century.

7. **Pyrrhic victory**

   Pyrrhus was so called because of his red or fiery beard. He was the impulsive, bull-headed type who rushes in or persists against his better judgment in a campaign he cannot win.

8. **stygian**

   A Stygian oath was one that could not be broken because it was sworn by the river Styx. The myths of the river Styx come to us chiefly from the Odyssey of Homer and from Virgil's *Aeneid*.

9. **tantalizing**

   *Tantalum* is a metal so named because it proved so difficult to extract. It is used in nuclear reactors, aircraft, and surgical instruments because of its extremely high melting point (2996°C) and its very great resistance to corrosion.

10. **terpischorean**

    Dance words of yesteryear include *bolero, fandango, cancan, minuet, waltz, polka, gavotte, mazurka, ballet,* etc. Elicit from the students a list of today's dance words.

11. **Titanic**

    *Titanium* is a dark gray or silvery metal with a melting point of 1675°C, used in satellites as well as in aircraft. *Titan* words include *titanosaur*, a large dinosaur, and the diminutive name of *Titania*, queen of fairyland.

# KEYS

### First Practice Set*

1. aurora, paeans
2. Apollonian, Dionysian
3. Amazons, Valhalla
4. odyssey, aegis
5. plutocrat, palladium, ambrosial
6. siren, Pyrrhic
7. procrustean, promethean
8. terpsichorean, hermetic
9. tantalizing, plutocrat
10. stygian, titanic

### Second Practice Set

1. ambrosial, aegis, Amazons
2. Elysian fields, aurora
3. Paradiso, Apollonian
4. procrustean, Pyrrhic victory, Titan
5. terpsichorean, stygian
6. tantalizing, hermetic
7. Promethean, Paradise
8. odyssey, Dionysian
9. plutocrat, palladium, paean

### Third Practice Set

**A.**

1. 3
2. 8
3. 1
4. 11
5. 10
6. 5
7. 2
8. 12
9. 6
10. 7

**B.**

1. 6
2. 11
3. 1
4. 12
5. 8
6. 2
7. 10
8. 7
9. 5
10. 4

## Unit Test  (Word Wealth Testing Program)

1. w (plutocrat);  t (siren)
2. b (Apollonian);  q (palladium)
3. x (aegis);  s (aurora)
4. p (Amazons);  u (odyssey)
5. l (Dionysian); e (terpsichorean)
6. v (paean);  y (aureole)
7. f (Procrustean);  h (Pyrrhic)
8. a (Promethean);  d (titanic)
9. o (Valhalla);  j (bacchanalian)
10. i (ambrosial);  k (stygian)
11. r (Elysium);  n (aeonian); m (hermetic)
12. g (aeolian);  c (aureate)

---

*Inform your pupils as they begin this test that one word is used twice (the word *plutocrat* in sentences 5 and 9).

# part two

## unit one

### CAVEAT EMPTOR

1. corroborate (them)  2. dubious  3. acquiesce  4. depreciate
5. internal  6. dilate  7. abridge  8. discriminate
9. indulgent  10. livid

### VERBS

**1. abridge**

It is advisable to bring in *epitome,* a short statement of the main points but more often used to denote a part (or person) which well represents the whole: "Jefferson was the *epitome* of early American political genius." A *composite* photograph or figure combines typical elements to produce a whole that is perfectly representative of the various components. The *quintessence* is the pure essence of something.

**2. acquiesce**

*Quiescent* (quiet, inactive, latent) may be discussed.

**3. allude**

The –lude– words are presented on p. 280 of *Word Wealth.* See also *delusion* (WW p. 106 under *illusion*) and *collusion* (WW p. 181 under *collaborate*).

**4. constitute**

*Comprise* (consist of) is a synonym: "Nine justices, each appointed for life, *comprise* (or *constitute*) the Supreme Court." *Include, comprehend,* and *embrace* are similar in meaning.

**5. contrive**

The root is Old French: *trover,* to find.

**6. corroborate**

The meaning of the Latin root, *roborare,* is to strengthen. It is helpful to show why the *r* is doubled in *corroborate.*

### 7. culminate

*Column* ultimately comes from the same Latin root, *culmen*, peak or summit.

### 8. depreciate

This word stays close to the meaning of its root, *pretiare*, to value, and *pretium*, price. The person form, *depreciator*, is sometimes used.

### 9. dilate

Joseph Conrad is particularly fond of this word. It comes from Latin *dilatare*, to spread out, from dis–, apart, plus *latus*, wide. (The word *dilatory*, characterized by delay, on the other hand, comes from the Latin *ferre, latus*, to carry, a very large family presented on p. 297 of WW.)

### 10. discriminate

This word has come to imply unjust or unfair action based on distinctions of race, color, or creed. That, however, is a specialized use. The Latin root, *crimen*, verdict, is the root also of *incriminate* and *recriminate*.

## ADJECTIVES

### 1. arid

The Latin root *aridus* also means dry.

### 2. chronic

Compare *inveterate* (WW p. 116) used chiefly of habits or tastes. *Chronic* is mostly used of illness or complaints. It comes from the Greek word element –chron–, time, presented with the Latin –temp– (WW p. 341).

### 3. dubious

*Dubiety* is a state of doubt or uncertainty. *Conviction, certainty,* and *assurance* might be mentioned as antonyms of the noun form.

### 4. indulgent

The Latin root, *indulgēre*, to be kind, to yield, gives the word an ironic flavor. Antonyms of *indulgence* include *discipline, restraint,* and *rigor*.

### 5. internal

*Extern* is a recognized word for a nonresident doctor, and *externalize* is the counterpart of *internalize*.

## 6. lethal

The Latin root is *lethum*, death. *Lethe* was the river of forgetfulness in Hades from which a person drank before returning for another life on earth. The root of Lethe is the Greek word *lethe*, forgetfulness or oblivion, and is thus closely related in meaning and form to the Latin word, *lethum*.

## 7. livid

*Lividity* is associated with rage, fear, or emotional states; *pallidness* (pallor) connotes ill health, fatigue, or mental strain; and *wan* is a sympathetic word applied to persons in poor health.

## 8. overt

It is a strong word, almost as strong as *intrusive*. It comes from the French word *ouvrir*, to open, and thus is not one of the –vert– (turn) words or a variant of *over*.

## 9. senile

*Senescence* is the process of becoming old, especially of people, whereas *obsolescence* is applied to machines and equipment. *Geriatrics*, the branch of medicine that deals with the ailments and hygiene of old age, has become a familiar specialty in medicine. Compare *pediatrics*, the medical care of children.

## 10. virtual

Like *virtue, virtuous, virtuoso,* and *virtuosity, virtual* comes from the Latin *virtus*, strength, virtue. It has a noun form, *virtuality*, essence, potential existence.

# KEYS

**First Practice Set**

1. allude, contrived
2. discriminate, lethal
3. chronic, arid
4. acquiesce, virtual
5. abridge, depreciate
6. indulgent, dilated
7. corroborate, senile
8. culminate, overt
9. internal, livid
10. constitute, dubious

**Second Practice Set**

1. accede to, synopsis
2. assent, concur
3. livid, longevity
4. dotage, superannuation
5. humid, sear
6. compendium, manifest
7. constituent, abstract
8. digest, conspicuous
9. sterile, senile dementia
10. ostensible, palpable

## Third Practice Set

1. b (dissent)
2. c (life-giving)
3. a (grow narrow)
4. a (lengthen)
5. e (actual)
6. d (unyielding)
7. a (humid)
8. b (increase in value)
9. d (hidden)
10. c (youthful)

## The Correct Choice

**A.**
1. 3
2. 9
3. 5
4. 11
5. 2
6. 12
7. 1
8. 6
9. 4
10. 7

**B.**
1. 4
2. 8
3. 1
4. 9
5. 6
6. 2
7. 10
8. 12
9. 11
10. 5

## Unit Test  *(Word Wealth Testing Program)*

1. f (senile);  a (indulgent)
2. c (dubious);  u (culminate)
3. z (concur);  y (assent)
4. m (dubitable);  j (chronic)
5. g (manifest);  i (palpable)
6. o (livid);  cc (dilate)
7. w (accede);  aa (abridge)
8. bb (discriminate); q (abstract);  s (digest)
9. e (lethal);  k (desiccated)
10. p (summit);  d (conspicuous)
11. n (sterile);  b (internal)
12. l (ostensible);  v (corroborate)

# unit two

## PARTY

| | | | |
|---|---|---|---|
| 1. accelerate | 2. simulate | 3. similes | 4. exaggerate |
| 5. recuperate, resuscitate | 6. jeopardize, moron | 7. humiliate | 8. impale |
| 9. tenacity | 10. scroll, promulgate | 11. improvise, metaphors | 12. nonentity |

## VERBS

### 1. accelerate

*Decelerate* is the closest antonym. *Accelerator* is the agent form.

### 2. compensate

*Remuneration* might also be mentioned. A *compensated* balance wheel in a clock or watch has bimetallic strips which counteract temperature changes. Such a device is one kind of *compensator*.

### 3. exaggerate

The root is *agger*, a heap or mound in Latin, but the word is not to be confused with *aggregate* or *aggregation*, which come from *gregare*, to lead in a herd.

### 4. humiliate

*Degrade, disgrace, dishonor,* and *abase* are synonyms.

### 5. impale

The Latin root is *palus*, a pole or stake. In heraldry, to *impale* is to connect or place two coats of arms side by side on a single shield.

### 6. jeopardize

*Peril* is somewhat more specific and more immediate than *jeopardy*. *Hazard*, on the other hand, is less imminent and more abstract than *jeopardy* and more categorical. Ancient peoples feared the *perils* of the sea, and they put their lives in *jeopardy* whenever they set sail. Sea travel was one of the *hazards* they had to face to sell goods or explore their world.

7. **perpetrate**

The root of *perpetrate* is Latin *patrare,* to bring about, accomplish. (The word has no connection with *perpetual,* which comes from *perpetuus,* constant.) *Enact,* a related word meaning to do or accomplish something, may be mentioned. It is used chiefly of drama, pantomime, or acts of a legislature.

8. **promulgate**

This word comes from Latin *promulgare,* to proclaim, thought to be, perhaps, an alteration of Latin *provulgare,* from *vulgare,* to publish, and thus traceable to *vulgus,* the people. *Divulge,* to disclose (WW p. 4), is more clearly a derivative of *vulgus.*

9. **resuscitate**

The agent word *resuscitator* may be mentioned and also the less-frequent adjective form, *resuscitative.*

10. **simulate**

From its root, Latin *simulare,* to imitate, from *similis,* like, similar, come also *simulacrum* (vague likeness, pretense, counterfeit), and *dissimulation* (deception), an older word much used in the seventeenth century and sometimes today. *Similar* and other simil– words come more directly from the Latin adjective, *similis,* like. *Simultaneous* is derived from Latin simul–, at the same time, which also comes from *similis,* same, similar.

# NOUNS

1. **metaphor**

The Greek root *pherein,* to carry, and meta–, beyond, faithfully indicate the way in which a metaphor carries one beyond the actual, literal, present frame of reference to create an implied comparison with something of a different class or kind.

2. **moron**

*Dolt, nincompoop, zany, imbecile* are related words.

3. **nonentity**

The root is *esse,* the Latin verb to be, which is also the source of *essence, essential,* and their variants. The word *entity,* which means being or existence, also has a technical meaning in philosophy. Thus *nonentity* means a person or thing which has no real or mental existence.

4. **parity**

A person not up to *par* is not equal to his own normal level.

5. **satellite**

   *Satellite,* a French-derived word, came in turn from the Latin *satelles, satellitis,* an attendant or guard.

6. **scroll**

   *Scroll* also means a list or schedule. Its Old French root, *escroue,* a roll of writings, of Germanic origin, is the root also of *escrow,* a term for the process by which papers, funds, or property are put in the hands of a third party until all conditions are met for transferring possession.

7. **simile**

   See the preceding notes on the words *simulate* and *metaphor.*

8. **sovereign**

   Quite by accident *sovereign* contains the word *reign.* The Latin root is super–, above or over, from Old French via Middle English.

9. **stratum**

   Such words as *datum, erratum, desideratum, maximum, medium,* and *minimum* may be mentioned—words that come directly from Latin and retain the neuter spellings of the third declension in both singular and plural. *Ultimatum* and *arboretum* also form a plural in *a,* but *s* is their preferred ending.

10. **tenacity**

    The Latin root, *tenere,* is presented as the word element –tain–, –ten(t)– on p. 298 of *Word Wealth* with thirteen of its more immediate derivatives.

# KEYS

## First Practice Set

1. perpetrated, resuscitate
2. compensate, humiliate
3. simulate, impale
4. metaphor, satellite
5. nonentity, moron
6. parity, simile
7. exaggerate, jeopardize
8. tenacity, accelerate
9. sovereign, scroll
10. stratum, promulgate

## Second Practice Set

1. manifesto, grandioseness
2. caricature, proclamation
3. bruit, prosecute
4. simulate, perseverance
5. obstinacy, transact
6. disseminate, pronouncement
7. maneuver, recompense
8. persistence, recuperate
9. encyclical, propagate
10. evolve, velocity

## Third Practice Set

1. 7
2. 8
3. 6
4. 5
5. 1
6. 2
7. 7
8. 3

## Antonyms

1. d (minimize)
2. a (make proud)
3. b (retard)
4. c (celebrity)
5. a (inequality)
6. e (slave)
7. b (suppress)
8. d (intelligent)
9. c (literal)
10. a (laxity)

## Similarities and Differences

1. The list includes *decelerate, uncompensated, unexaggerated, unhumiliated, unimpaled, unjeopardized, unperpetrated, unpromulgated, unresuscitated, unsimulated.*
2. Impale, impalement.

## Share and Share Alike

1. red
2. stiff
3. bare
4. baked
5. instant
6. gold
7. common
8. French
9. ill
10. low
11. clean
12. slippery
13. sliding
14. slow
15. well
16. lonely
17. blood
18. Italian
19. silver
20. high
21. dead
22. merry
23. double
24. Persian
25. bottom
26. high
27. dry
28. animal
29. second
30. rugged

## Another Word Game

1. starboard
2. violin
3. busby
4. caret
5. coloratura

## Unit Test  (Word Wealth Testing Program)

1. a (metaphor);  f (moron)
2. j (perseverance); b (persistence)
3. w (simulate);  m (impalement)
4. d (nonentity);  t (transact)
5. i (edict);  c (manifesto)
6. y (bruit);  k (stratum)
7. r (disseminate); v (promulgate)
8. o (satellite);  e (velocity)
9. h (hyperbole);  q (simile)
10. s (accelerate);  x (expedite)
11. aa (perpetrate);  u (humiliate)
12. g (tenacity);  cc (resuscitate); z (indemnify)

# unit three

## WOULD BE

1. d (a likeness)
2. b (a crossbred plant)
3. c (a tyrant)
4. a (an attraction)
5. b (abundance)
6. c (easy)
7. b (impulsive)
8. b (chastise)
9. c (exactness)
10. a (closeness)

## NOUNS

1. **affinity**

   This word contains the familiar –fini(t)– element, meaning end (see WW p. 351 with –termin–).

2. **despot**

   *Despot* is probably the most contemptuous term available for a strong ruler because the sound of the word implies more scorn than *tyrant,* though the denotative meaning of the two words is the same. The word comes, via Old French, from the Greek *despotes,* a lord or master.

3. **effigy**

   The –fing–, –fig– element from the Latin verb *fingere,* to shape or form, appears in *effigy,* also in *figure* and its variants.

4. **hybrid**

   The Latin root, *hybrida,* denotes the progeny of a tame sow and a wild boar. *Hybridism* and *hybridization* may also be mentioned. The mule is an example of the latter.

5. **illusion**

   The word is built from the element –lus– (WW p. 280). Its meaning needs to be clearly distinguished from that of *allusion* (WW p. 87), built from the same root but with a different prefix.

6. **opulence**

   *Opulence* comes from the Latin *ops, opis,* might or wealth, and is not related to *opus,* a work or piece of work.

## 7. precision

*Precision* is one of the numerous words based on the root –cide–, –cis– (WW p. 332), but not one for which the root meaning is strikingly different.

## 8. proximity

The root is the Latin superlative, *proximus,* nearest. *Proximate* (next or nearest) and *proximal* (an anatomical term) are sometimes used.

## 9. reminiscence

The root, meaning to remember again (from *memini,* to remember), appears in *memento* and *memorandum.* From a variant form in Latin (*memoria,* a memory) come *memoir* and other *memory* words.

## 10. reprisal

A somewhat grimmer word than *retaliation, reprisal* derives from the same root as *reprehend,* i.e., *reprehendere,* to seize again. *Reprieve* comes from *reprendere,* to take back.

# ADJECTIVES

## 1. adroit

The French root, *droit,* right, suggests the superior skill of the right hand over the left, but actually it denotes *moral* right. *Deft* and *dexterous* are synonyms of *adroit.*

## 2. facile

The verb form, *facilitate,* is widely used.

## 3. feline

*Leonine* may be added to the list. Also *aquiline* (like an eagle), applied especially to a nose shaped like an eagle's beak; and *soricine* (shrewish and thus fond of nagging or scolding) may be mentioned.

## 4. mediocre

A French word imported bodily, it has never adapted itself to English ways of spelling. The root meaning in Latin is middle peak, and medi(o)– from the Latin *medius,* middle, is a word element found in *medium, mediate,* and a number of other English words.

5. **prodigious**

   *Prodigal* from Latin *prodigere,* to drive forth or away (from normal ways of behaving), from pro–, prod–, forth, plus *agere,* to drive, means extremely generous, profuse, or wasteful.

6. **prosaic**

   *Unpoetic, commonplace, uninspired,* and *lackluster* are synonyms, and even *pedestrian,* in the sense of slow, dull, uninspired, even-paced, and monotonous.

7. **punitive**

   Related words range from *disciplinary,* which may imply punishment, to *retaliatory,* which implies revenge as much as it does justice or punishment. *Punitive* serves as an adjective form for *chasten* and *chastise.*

8. **spontaneous**

   The Latin root, *sponte,* of one's free will, is not to be confused with *spondere,* to promise, from which come *despond(ent), respond, correspond, responsible,* and other –spond–, –sponse– words. Related words include *instinctive, voluntary,* and *automatic.*

9. **subtle**

   The implications of the word are often evil, especially when applied to Satan or any kind of malefactor. The Latin root word *tela,* web, supports this implication. The verb *subtilize* retains the *i* that *subtle* once had.

10. **transient**

    The root is *ire,* to go, as in *transitive, transit, transition,* and their numerous variants. See the prefix trans– (WW p. 278). *Momentary* may be added to the list of related words.

# KEYS

## First Practice Set

1. spontaneous, hybrid
2. affinity, illusion
3. effigy, mediocre
4. opulence, transient
5. reprisals, precision
6. proximity, reminisce
7. despot, subtle
8. adroit, facile
9. punitive, prosaic
10. feline, prodigious

80/part two

**Second Practice Set**

1. viceroy, hallucination
2. mannequin, counterpart
3. retrospect, memoirs
4. replica, commemorate
5. memento, counterfeit
6. potentate, vulpine
7. delusion, affluent
8. vengeance, impunity
9. icon, facsimiles
10. memorabilia, porcine

**The Right Word**

A.

1. 4
2. 10
3. 7
4. 12
5. 8
6. 6
7. 9
8. 2
9. 11
10. 1

B.

1. 7
2. 10
3. 9
4. 8
5. 11
6. 2
7. 6
8. 4
9. 5
10. 1

**Tangents**

1. It was once believed that one could injure or destroy an enemy by making a likeness and burning it. From this practice of folk magic comes the custom of hanging a person in effigy or burning a likeness as a demonstration of popular hatred or disapproval.

2. *As gentle as a kitten.* Strands of meaning: soft, furry, cuddly, graceful, delicate.
   *As cruel as a cat catching a mouse.* Strands of meaning: sharp claws, tormenting, ruthless manner of cat; painful, suffering, helpless mouse.
   A *lycanthrope* is a wolf man, a werewolf, or an insane person who imagines himself to be a wolf. *Lycanthropy* is wolflike behavior because of insanity or one's nature.

3. The Latin root from which it comes, *(h)allucinari,* means to wander mentally. *Hallucinogens* are drugs, such as mescaline, peyote, and LSD, that produce hallucinations.

4. *Bovine, simian,* and *asinine* indicate animal qualities or behavior. *Senile* and *puerile* indicate childishness. All imply behavior below the norm.

## Unit Test   *(Word Wealth Testing Program)*

1. ff (chieftain);   t (despot)
2. p (opulence);   i (illusive)
3. z (mediocrity);   g (bovine)
4. r (adroitness);   cc (precision)
5. b (evanescent);
   gg (retrospection)
6. aa (facility);   ee (delusion)
7. v (counterpart);   k (asinine)
8. s (hybrid);   m (vulpine);
   e (lupine)
9. o (prodigious);
   d (spontaneous)
10. dd (effigy);   w (facsimile)
11. x (replica);   y (impunity)
12. u (potentate);   c (simian)

# unit four

## ADJECTIVITIS

1. c (quick to complain)
2. b (commonplace)
3. d (hard to interpret)
4. c (subject to whims)
5. b (horrible)
6. a (dismal)
7. c (firmly established)
8. b (eager)
9. d (stern and sober)
10. b (painstaking)

## ADJECTIVES

1. **austere**

   The word, which came into English from Old French, is derived from Latin *austerus*, from Greek *austēros*, from *auein*, to parch, to dry.

2. **avid**

   This word comes from the same Latin verb as *avaricious*, namely, *avere*, to desire, to crave.

3. **capricious**

   The word, which derives from the Italian *capriccioso*, can be traced to the Latin *caper*, goat. *Fickle, inconstant,* and *unstable* are related words, although none is a true synonym. *Vagary* is a near synonym for *caprice*, but a *caprice* is light and playful in its connotations, and *vagary* implies seriousness, vagueness, or confusion.

4. **competent**

   The word, derived from the Latin *petere*, to seek, is actually an adjective form of *compete*, thus it means able or worthy to compete. *Inept* and, of course, *incompetent* are good antonyms.

5. **diffident**

   The word means, literally, away from or lack of (dis–) trust (–fid–), in this case lack of trust or faith in oneself. For other words from –fid(e)– see Word Wealth p. 361.

## 6. diminutive

In root meaning and effect *diminutive* is an adjective form of *diminish*. Inasmuch as *diminish* is not an entry word, it is desirable to bring in *diminution* (lessening or decreasing) and perhaps *diminuendo,* a musical term for gradual decrease in loudness.

## 7. formidable

The accent is on the first syllable. The Latin root is *formido,* fear, and *fearsome* is an acceptable synonym, though *formidable* implies something difficult to accomplish or overcome, not something one fears.

## 8. inexorable

*Exorable,* the positive form, is less familiar. The Latin root, *orare,* to beg or pray, is the root also of *oration* and of *orisons* (prayers), a word used by Hamlet speaking to Ophelia: "Maiden, in thy *orisons* be all my sins remembered."

## 9. inscrutable

The Latin root, *scrutari,* to search out, is the root also of *scrutinize* (WW p. 141) and *scrutiny*. Its positive form is *scrutable.*

## 10. inveterate

*Veteran* comes from the same Latin root, *veterus,* old.

## 11. lugubrious

The Latin root *lugere,* to mourn, is akin to the Greek *lygros,* mournful.

## 12. melancholy

Historically thought to be the product of black bile (the Greek *chole*), *melancholy* is naturally associated with dark colors, especially black. <u>Melan–</u> means black in such words as *Melanesia, melanin* (pigment found in skin and hair), and *melanite* (a black kind of garnet). *Melancholia,* as mental disorder, and *melancholiac,* one so disordered, go beyond mere melancholy.

## 13. meticulous

From the Latin adjective, *meticulosus,* fearful, from *metus,* fear, the word has come to indicate the painstakingness that results from fear rather than the fear itself.

## 14. munificent

The Latin root, *munus,* gift or service, links *munificent* with *common* and *community,* which have been traced to the same root, but not with *munition* or *muniment,* which come from *munire,* to fortify.

## 15. opportune

One of the less rewarding derivatives of *portus,* a harbor or haven, it nevertheless evokes the picture of a ship near port, actually before or against the port (ob–) and thus readily available.

## 16. plebeian

The Latin root means the common people, the *plebs* as they were called in Rome. The patricians were the aristocratic class.

## 17. precipitous

The word is traceable to Latin *praecipitis,* headlong. Its use is largely literal, while the use of *precipitate* (quick to act) as an adjective is rather literary and *precipitate* as a verb is abstract but dramatic. In chemistry, *precipitate* denotes what settles to the bottom in a solution.

## 18. precocious

The root is *coquere,* to cook, but to cook means to mature, and thus the word comes to mean mature ahead of the time expected (*pre-*). The immediate Latin root, *praecox,* early ripe, is the word which appears in the phrase *dementia praecox,* the madness of youth. It came into use because the incidence of schizophrenia and other kinds of insanity was so high in young people about twenty years old.

## 19. pugnacious

A *litigious* person is eager to fight court battles and lawsuits. *Pugilism,* as the art or practice of boxing, may also be mentioned.

## 20. querulous

The word suggests mournful, acidulous complaint, not irritability as such or spitefulness and ill humor. It has been traced to the Latin verb *queri,* to complain.

# KEYS

### First Practice Set

1. inexorable, lugubrious
2. opportune, austere
3. competent, capricious
4. inveterate, formidable

5. diffident, meticulous
6. querulous, pugnacious
7. melancholy, inscrutable
8. precocious, munificent
9. avid, precipitous
10. diminutive, plebeian

**Second Practice Set**
1. sobriety, asceticism
2. erratic, proficiency
3. adroitness, petulant
4. punctiliousness, mania
5. despondency, combative
6. ardor, rapacity
7. lachrymose, finesse
8. disconsolate, despair
9. dejection, morbid
10. spasmodic, precipitate

**Third Practice Set**

A.
1. 10
2. 12
3. 8
4. 7
5. 3
6. 11
7. 4
8. 5
9. 1
10. 2

B.
1. 11
2. 7
3. 8
4. 9
5. 1
6. 3
7. 12
8. 4
9. 2
10. 6

**Antonyms**
1. c (happy)
2. b (consistent)
3. b (yielding)
4. d (stingy)
5. b (oversized)
6. a (self-indulgent)
7. a (uncomplaining)
8. d (ill-timed)
9. c (cheerful)
10. b (easy to overcome)

**Explorations**

1. belli–   from Latin *bellum*, war
   dur–    from Latin *durare*, to last, harden, with some influence of Latin *durus*, hard, in *durable*
   melan–  from Greek *melanos*, black
   pugn–   from Latin *pugnare*, to fight
   punc(t)– from Latin *punctum*, point

2. *Couplet, eyelet, gimlet, inlet, playlet, quadruplet, quintuplet, triplet* are among the possibilities.

3. The root of *patrician* is –patri– (WW p. 314), specifically *patres*, fathers or senators. For the root of *precocious*, see p. 83 of this manual. *Morbid* comes from Latin *morbidus*, diseased, from *morbus*, disease.

## Unit Test   *(Word Wealth Testing Program)*

1. ee (austerity);  y (despondency)
2. w (avidity);  u (covetousness)
3. j (meticulous);  c (punctual)
4. l (petulant);  k (querulous)
5. f (opportune);  p (formidable)
6. s (asceticism);  m (lugubrious)
7. dd (sobriety);  o (inveterate); t (competence)
8. d (melancholy); q (lachrymose)
9. b (wistful);  g (diminutive)
10. z (precocity);  h (precipitate)
11. n (belligerent); x (inscrutability)
12. i (chronic);  e (capricious)

# unit five

## DO YOU?

1. c (pay it out)
2. b (implicate him)
3. a (call him before a court)
4. d (infringe)
5. c (insurance)
6. a (loss)
7. d (a choice)
8. a (state it)
9. d (defame that person)
10. c (a statement of indebtedness)

## VERBS OF BUSINESS AND LAW

1. **allege**

   *Allege, allegiance,* and *allegory* all come from different roots, *allege* being from the Latin verb *litigare,* to dispute, the root of *litigate.* Synonyms include *affirm, insist, avouch, asseverate.*

2. **arraign**

   *Accuse, challenge, indict,* and *impeach* are related words. To *indict* is to charge a person formally with a crime. To *impeach* is to challenge or discredit, especially the holder of a high public office. The root of *arraign* is *ratio,* reason, reckoning.

3. **bequeath**

   The root in this case is the Old English *cwethan,* to say, which is also the root of *quoth. Bespeak,* also from Old English, is a synonym, as far as a technical word like *bequeath* can have one.

4. **disburse**

   The root is French, *bourse,* from Latin *bursa.* Both words mean purse.

5. **encroach**

   The root is the French *croche,* a hook. It is the root also of the word *crochet.*

6. **exonerate**

   The word means literally to take the load (or weight) from someone, the root being the Latin noun *onus,* a weight or burden.

7. **incriminate**

See notes on *discriminate* on p. 70 of this manual.

## NOUNS OF BUSINESS AND LAW

1. **actuary**

   *Interact* and *react* may be added to the "act" words. Three of them have agent forms: *actuator, activator, reactor.*

2. **alibi**

   *Alibi* comes from the Latin phrase *alius ibi,* somewhere else.

3. **debenture**

   The word took its rise from a Latin phrase with which statements of indebtedness once began, *debentur mihi,* there are owing to me. In a similar way, writs of *habeus corpus* and of *mandamus* came to be known by their opening words.

4. **increment**

   *Increment* comes from the Latin *incrementum,* an increase. The word *decrement* has a limited use, especially for waste or the amount that is lost thereby. An *increscent* moon is increasing; a *decrescent* moon is waning. An *excrescence* is any outgrowth.

5. **libel**

   The Latin root *libellus* means a little book. In late seventeenth-century England, libels were lampoons written on sheets of paper and passed around anonymously in the coffeehouses.

6. **litigation**

   See *allege* p. 85 of this manual. Due process (of law) is another term for litigation.

7. **option**

   Other words for a choice include *alternative* and *preference* (WW p. 114).

8. **solvency**

   It is one of the –solve–, –solu(t)– words (see WW p. 290).

## NOUNS—FUNERAL WORDS

1. **bereavement**

   Be– is an Old English prefix which in this case intensifies the meaning of –reave–, from Middle English *reve(n)*, Old English *reāfian*, to seize or rob. Compare *beget, beguile, bemuse*.

2. **condolence**

   The Latin root *dolere*, to grieve, appears in *dole, doleful,* and *indolent*. But *redolent* comes from *olere*, to smell.

3. **dirge**

   The word comes from *dirige*, direct thou (imperative of *dirigere*) as the opening word of Psalm 5:8, used in the Latin Office for the Burial of the Dead. *Lament* and *lamentation* are related words.

4. **epitaph**

   *Cenotaph* (empty tomb) comes from the same Greek root, *taphos*, a tomb.

5. **interment**

   The root of *inter* and *interment* is *terra*, earth. Not so with *deter*, however. Its root is *terrere*, to frighten or terrify.

## KEYS

**First Practice Set**

1. litigation, libel
2. debentures, increment
3. arraigned, alibi
4. epitaph, interment
5. exonerate, disbursed
6. alleges, encroaches
7. solvency, actuaries
8. dirges, condolence
9. bequeath, bereavement
10. option, incriminating

**Second Practice Set**

1. bursar, fiscal, deficit
2. acquit, recriminations, prosecutor
3. cremated, requiem, cenotaph
4. commiseration, compassion
5. intrude, invasion of, infringement
6. exhume, sarcophagus
7. defamation, calumny
8. libel, obituary

**Third Practice Set**

1. 10
2. 7
3. 6
4. 8
5. 11
6. 12
7. 9
8. 2
9. 5
10. 4

## For Practice

1. *Habeas corpus* means literally, "You have (or hold) the body" (*i.e.*, person). These are the opening words of the legal document used to bring an accused before a court.
   *Mandamus*, meaning "we command or enjoin," is the opening word of a court order requiring the performance of some obligation clearly specified by law.
   *Certiorari*, meaning "to be informed," is a writ by which a superior court calls for the records of a case or proceedings of a lower court or body.

2. The noun forms of the verbs listed under *encroach* are *invasion, infringement, presumption,* and *arrogance* or *arrogation* (a legal term for assuming a role that belongs to the courts).

3. The depth words and their most familiar variant forms include:

   felony—felonious
   imprison—imprisonment
   arraignment—arraign
   allege—allegation
   detention—detain
   bail—bailment, bailiff, bailable
   docket—(no variant forms)
   prosecutor—prosecute, prosecution
   verdict—(no variant forms)
   acquit—acquittal
   convict—conviction
   sentence—sentential (seldom used)
   intestate—intestable, intestacy
   probate—probation, probationer, probative
   disburse—disbursement
   expend—expenditure
   pay—payment, payee
   reimburse—reimbursement
   bourse—(no variant forms)
   bursar—bursary, bursarship
   invade—invasion
   infringe—infringement
   presume—presumption
   arrogate—arrogation
   absolve—absolution
   aquit—aquittal
   exculpate—exculpation
   discrimination—discriminate

recrimination—recriminate
actuate—actuation
actualize—actualization
activate—activation
counteract—counteraction
alibi—(no variant forms)
debit—debitable
deficit—(no variant forms)
appreciation—appreciate, appreciable (assets)
defamation—defame, defamatory
slander—slanderous
calumny—calumniate
derogation—derogatory
disparagement—disparage
prerogative—(no variant forms)
liability—liable
fiscal—fiscally
compassion—compassionate
commiseration—commiserate
requiem—requiscat (a prayer for the repose of the dead)
obituary—obituarize, obituarist
necrology—necrologist
mausoleum—mausolean (seldom used)
sepulcher—sepulchral, sepulture
cenotaph—(no variant forms)
sarcophagus—sarcophagous, sarcophagy
cremation—cremate, crematorium, crematory
bequeath—bequest
disinter—disinterment
exhume—exhumation

4. The meanings are:

prosecute—to follow forth or in behalf of, especially a legal authority or court
disburse—to get money paid out or "apart" from its source
debenture—amount owed (from *debére,* to owe)
verdict—said truly (Latin *verus* plus *dit,* a saying), *i.e.,* a legal truth
exonerate—to take the weight (*onus*) from
solvent—loosening substance
epitaph—upon a tomb
sarcophagus—flesh-eating (because limestone coffins had a disintegrating effect on the body inside)
condolence—feeling sorrow or grief with (someone), *i.e.,* sympathy
interment—(act of) placing in the ground or earth (*terra*)
dissection—(act of) cutting apart

## Unit Test  (*Word Wealth Testing Program*)

1. bb (allege);  c (infringement)
2. i (felony);  o (arraignment)
3. u (disburse);  x (bequeath)
4. y (absolve);  cc (acquit); t (exculpate)
5. f (litigation);  r (libel)
6. dd (incriminate);  aa (exhume)
7. v (arrogate);  a (alibi)
8. k (bereavement); e (condolence)
9. q (necrology);  h (requiem)
10. d (epitaph);  s (interment)
11. g (debenture);  l (solvency)
12. j (disparagement or derogation);  p (calumny)

# unit six

## STANCES

1. c (assess it)
2. a (an apparition)
3. c (duplicity)
4. d (an alien)
5. d (a clairvoyant)
6. b (cajolery)
7. d (extort it)
8. a (abstinence)
9. b (an altercation)
10. a (an assessment)
11. c (a concession)
12. b (a poltergeist)
13. d (a conflagration)
14. a (acerbity)
15. c (patronizing)

## VERBS

1. **abstain**

   *Abstain* is one of the many –tain–, –ten(t)– words (WW p. 298) from the Latin *tenere*, to hold; the *s* goes with *ab–*.

2. **alienate**

   The word comes from *alius*, other. *Alienator* is the agent form, and *alienist* is an older word for a psychiatrist.

3. **assess**

   The root is the Latin verb *sedere*, to sit. *Asset, assiduity* (diligence, perseverance), and *assiduous* come from the same source.

4. **assimilate**

   Another word akin to *similis*, like, from Latin *simulare, similare*, to make similar. *Assimilate* has no precise synonym. *Homogenize* is close, but its meaning is to make something all of the same quality or consistency, whereas *assimilate* involves the process of incorporating something initially alien and is used chiefly of ideas or persons.

5. **cajole**

   *Cajole* comes from an Old French word, *cagaioler*, to allure wild birds into a cage with songbirds as decoys. *Cajolement* is the noun form.

6. **concede**

    The word belongs to the large and quite pervasive –cede–, –ceed–, –cess– family introduced on p. 279 of *Word Wealth*. *Cede* is a process by which land is transferred peacefully from one nation to another.

7. **condescend**

    The element *–scend–*, climb, appears in *Word Wealth* on p. 304.

8. **deprecate**

    The word is derived from Latin *deprecatus*, from de– away, plus *precari*, to pray. *Deprecator* is the agent form, and the adjective forms, *deprecable* and *deprecatory*, have occasional usefulness.

9. **dissipate**

    From the Latin *sipare*, to throw, the word literally means to throw something away. *Dissipator* is the person form.

10. **elicit**

    The word is derived from Latin *elicere*, to draw out or evoke, from *lacere*, to allure. *Licitus*, allowable, appears in *licit* and *illicit* (not lawful or allowable). *Licere*, to be permitted, is the root of *licentious* (given to loose, immoral living).

11. **emaciate**

    A word of specialized and precise meaning, *emaciate* is a derivative of *emaciare*, to make lean.

12. **exasperate**

    Not to be confused with words like *aspiration*, from *spirare*, to breathe, or with *asperse* and *aspersion*, from *spargere*, to sprinkle, *exasperate* comes from Latin *exasperatus*, the past participle of *exasperare*, from ex– plus *asper*, rough.

# NOUNS

1. **altercation**

    This is one of the alter– words (see WW p. 347). *Embroilment* (a confused quarrel) may be added to the forms of discord.

2. **anguish**

    This word comes from the Latin *angere*, to tighten or choke, a form of which is also the source of the word *anger*.

### 3. apparition

*Apparition* is derived from the Latin *apparēre*, to appear. *Revenant* (spirit coming back after death) and *wraith* (spectral appearance just before or after death) are other "ghost" words.

### 4. barrage

The word (from French *barrer*, to bar, from *barre*, bar) may also mean a dam or other barrier constructed in a stream or river.

### 5. clairvoyant

A French word which has been imported into English, it means literally clear-seeing. Thus *clairvoyance*, if genuine, belongs to the developing science of extrasensory perception called parapsychology.

### 6. duplicity

See *elicit*, p. 92 of this manual, and the –pli–, –plic– words (WW p. 340).

### 7. facade

Another French word, deriving from the same Latin source as *face*. Compare *facet* (phase, aspect, or one of the plane surfaces of a cut gem).

### 8. holocaust

Other words from *holo-* (whole, entire) include *holophrastic* (expressing an entire sentence or phrase in one word), and *holohedral*. *Holocaust* is derived ultimately from the Greek *holokauston*, burnt whole, from *kaiein*, to burn.

# KEYS

## First Practice Set

1. conceded, clairvoyants
2. assess, holocaust
3. abstain, anguish
4. deprecating, apparitions
5. elicit, cajole
6. barrage, exasperated
7. emaciated, alienated
8. assimilate, facade
9. condescend, duplicity
10. altercation, dissipation

## Second Practice Set

1. asperity, extract
2. blandishment, fracas
3. appraise, holograph
4. poltergeist, imbroglio
5. refrain, dissolute
6. ordeal, chagrin
7. agony, acerbity
8. banshee, tribulation
9. dissension, litigation
10. zombi, salvo

## The Right Word

1. 6
2. 8
3. 10
4. 1
5. 2
6. 11
7. 12
8. 5
9. 7
10. 4

## Extra Action

1. assimilate—Latin <u>ad</u>-, to, plus *similare*, to make similar
   cajole—Old French *cagaioler*, to use decoy birds to attract wild birds into a cage
   clairvoyant—French *clair*, clear (from Latin *clarus*) plus *voyant*, seeing (from Latin *videre*, to see)
   condescend—Latin *com*-, with, plus <u>de</u>-, down, plus *scendere*, to climb
   duplicity—Latin <u>duo</u>-, two, plus *plicare*, to fold
   incorporate—Latin <u>in</u>-, plus *corpus, corporis*, body
   patronize—Latin *pater*, father
   specter—Latin verb *spectare*, to look at, behold

## Unit Test  *(Word Wealth Testing Program)*

1. d (anguish); w (alienate)
2. bb (abstain); dd (concede)
3. a (clairvoyant); h (holocaust)
4. u (assimilate); l (blandishments)
5. b (facade); o (duplicity)
6. n (imbroglio); f (zombie)
7. r (poltergeist); k (fracas)
8. t (asperity); j (purgatory)
9. s (salvo); i (exasperation); x (forbear)
10. g (altercation); z (desist)
11. v (elicit); p (emaciation)
12. aa (deprecate); e (mortification)

# unit seven

## SITUATIONS

1. d (venerate)
2. a (iterative)
3. d (orthodox)
4. d (transfigured)
5. b (vicious)
6. c (ostracized)
7. b (vacillating)
8. a (mercenary)
9. c (articulate)
10. a (pious)
11. d (a counterfeit)
12. a (puerile)
13. c (covetousness)
14. b (livid)
15. b (penurious)
16. a (tautology)

## VERBS

1. **galvanize**

    *Simony* (the buying or selling of church offices, pardons, and gifts) is another example of a word derived from a person's name. Other words from a person's name, especially in science, include *farad* (unit of capacity) from Michael Faraday, *curie* (unit of radioactivity) from Madame Curie, *ohm* (unit of electrical resistance) from George Ohm, and *watt* (unit of electric power) from James Watt.

2. **iterate**

    The Latin root is *iterum,* again. *Iterant* (adjective) and *iterance* (noun) are sometimes used.

3. **nurture**

    The word comes from the same root (Latin *nutrire,* to nourish, to nurse) as *nurse, nursery,* and their variants.

4. **ostracize**

    The Greek root, *ostrakon,* a shell, was the object used in taking a vote of ostracism in ancient Athens. *Exclusion* is a milder word, and *expatriation* is a form of self-ostracism by which a person decides to live abroad indefinitely because he finds his own country for some reason uncongenial.

5. **prevaricate**

    The word, from Latin *praevaracari,* to walk crookedly, is, along with *fabricate,* a gentle synonym for *lying* and *deceit.*

### 6. scrutinize

See note on *inscrutable* on p. 82 of this manual.

### 7. transfigure

See note on *effigy* on p. 77 of this manual.

### 8. vacillate

The word is derived from Latin *vacillare,* to sway, waver. Compare *falter,* which indicates hesitation from physical weakness or fear. *Vacillation* is indecisiveness and thus more psychological than physical, though it may be partly a result of fear or physical weakness.

### 9. venerate

Hawthorne is fond of this word, and it occurs in *The Scarlet Letter* almost as frequently as *anguish,* another of his favorite words. *Venerate* comes from the Latin *venerari* and retains the original meaning.

### 10. vitiate

Instead of meaning to make alive, as it might appear to do, the root is *vitium,* a vice, and the literal meaning is to make vicious or evil.

## ADJECTIVES

### 1. articulate

*Articulation* is used of the process of adjusting the lower schools to the needs or demands of the higher. The basic meaning of *articulate* is jointed, however, and *articulation* once referred to the joining of boards by a carpenter or cabinetmaker. The word is derived from Latin *articulare,* to divide into joints, utter distinctly.

### 2. juvenile

*Juvenility, juvenescent* (becoming youthful), and *juvenescence* may be mentioned as variant forms. The word is derived from Latin *juvenis,* young.

### 3. lucrative

The root is *lucrum,* gain or riches. Compare *lucre* (money) used in a humorous or derogatory sense.

### 4. mercenary

The word comes from Latin *merces,* reward, hire. *Mercenariness* and *mercenarily* are forms sometimes used.

5. **pallid**

The root is Latin *pallere*, to become pale. *Pall* (to become tiresome) and *pall* (a dark covering) come from quite different sources. See notes on *appall*, p. 33 of this manual. *Palette* comes from *pala*, a shovel. *Paleo–* in such words as *paleolithic* means ancient.

6. **pious**

*Impious* and *impiety* are precise opposites of *pious* and *piety*. Compare *sanctimonious* (falsely, hollowly, or ostentatiously pious) (WW p. 362).

7. **provident**

Note that it is one of the –vide–, vis– words (WW p. 343) and has the literal meaning of seeing forth or ahead.

8. **tolerant**

This word has a secondary meaning—being capable of resisting, specifically a drug or shock. For example: "The patient has no *tolerance* for penicillin."

9. **turbulent**

–Turb– is introduced as a word element on p. 333 of *Word Wealth*.

10. **vicious**

See note on *vitiate* p. 96 of this manual.

# KEYS

## First Practice Set

1. iterated, articulate
2. galvanized, vicious
3. juvenile, prevaricate
4. tolerant, venerate
5. turbulent, vitiated
6. pallid, transfigured
7. scrutinize, pious
8. mercenary, lucrative
9. provident, nurture
10. vacillate, ostracized

## Second Practice Set

1. mendacity, perturb
2. puerile, transmute
3. perverted, debauchery
4. covetousness, cupidity
5. dissimulation, hypocrisy
6. cadaverous, ghastly
7. counterfeit, metamorphose
8. nefarious, forgery
9. tautology, depraved
10. perjury, diabolical

## Third Practice Set

1. b (bored)
2. d (enhance)
3. a (unremunerative)
4. a (virtuous)
5. e (truthfulness)
6. b (happy-go-lucky)
7. c (disrespect)
8. a (calm)
9. d (actively oppose)
10. a (disregard)

## The Right Word

1. 11
2. 12
3. 10
4. 2
5. 1
6. 3
7. 6
8. 7
9. 4
10. 8

## Replacements

1. expatriate
2. devout
3. turgid
4. galvanic
5. deport
6. metamorphosed
7. sallow
8. duplicity
9. intolerance
10. banish

## Unit Test  *(Word Wealth Testing Program)*

1. d (juvenile);  b (lucrative)
2. c (mercenary);  f (provident)
3. i (cadaverous);  e (pious);  h (venerable)
4. m (cupidity);  bb (deprave)
5. p (mendacity);  k (fabrication)
6. u (transfigure);  y (galvanize)
7. g (vicious);  x (ostracize)
8. w (tolerate);  cc (reiterate)
9. z (cherish);  s (expatriation)
10. o (perjury);  aa (pervert)
11. l (metamorphosis);  q (transmutation)
12. t (counterfeit);  n (forgery)

# unit eight

## FIND

1. veracity  2. subterfuge  3. ardent  4. retribution  5. indolence
6. fluctuation  7. morale  8. futile  9. civil  10. celestial

## ADJECTIVES

1. **ardent**

   The Latin root *ardere*, to burn, is similar in meaning to the root of *fervent*, from Latin *fervere*, to boil or glow. *Fervid* and *perfervid* may be added as related words.

2. **benign**

   The word comes from *bene*, well, and *genus*, type or kind.

3. **celestial**

   From Latin *caelestis*, heavenly, and *caelum*, sky or heaven, *celestial* has no variant forms. Related words from the same root include *celesta* (a musical instrument); *Celeste, Celia,* and *Celestine,* feminine names; and *celestite* (a white mineral).

4. **civil**

   The word is derived from Latin *civilis*, from *civis*, citizen. *Civic, civics,* and *civilize* may be included. Compare *uncivil* with *uncivic* as antonyms of *civil* and *civic* respectively.

5. **complacent**

   The root of *complacent, placere*, to please, appears also in *placid, implacable,* and *placebo* (something harmless a doctor gives a patient to satisfy him).

6. **credible**

   *Credence, credential, credit (able), credo, credulity,* and *creed* all come, like *credible*, from the Latin *credere*, to trust, believe.

## 7. culpable

*Inculpable* is an antonym. The root is Latin *culpare,* to blame, from *culpa,* fault.

## 8. eccentric

Other –centric– words: *geocentric, egocentric, concentric, epicentric.*

## 9. futile

The Latin root *futilis* designates that which pours out easily and is therefore worthless. It goes back to *fundere,* to pour out, melt.

## 10. incipient

*Percipient* and *perceptive* are, like *incipient,* derivatives of *capere,* to take, as are *deceive, deceptive, receive, receptive,* and *conceive.*

# NOUNS

## 1. fallacy

The Latin root is *fallere,* to deceive.

## 2. fluctuation

The Latin root, *fluctus,* is traced to *fluere,* to flow. From this come the –flu–, –flux– words (WW p. 333). *Variation* is a synonym, but *fluctuation* indicates an ebb or flow, whereas *variation* may be any kind of change, regular or irregular. *Vicissitudes* are fluctuations in fortunes or affairs.

## 3. indolence

See note under *condolence* on p. 87 of this manual. The sense of *indolence* is not caring (literally, not grieving) about anything.

## 4. inference

This word is one of the less obvious derivatives of the Latin verb *ferre,* to bring. The –fer–, –late– elements (WW p. 297) come from the same root. *Inferable* and *inferential* are two of the less frequent forms of *infer.*

## 5. morale

The word is French, the feminine form of *moral.*

unit eight/101

6. **retribution**

    The root word, Latin *tribuere,* to pay, bestow, is the root also of *tribute* and *tributary. Tribe* and *tribune,* however, are derived from Latin *tribus,* one third of the Roman people, division of the people, tribe. And *tribulation* comes, ultimately, from *tribulum,* a threshing instrument.

7. **subterfuge**

    The Latin root *fugere,* to escape, appears in *fugitive* and numerous other words pertaining to fleeing or escaping. The sense of *subterfuge* is thus to escape (trouble) by something underhanded.

8. **temerity**

    The adjective *temerarious* is not often used.

9. **utility**

    *Utilization* and *utilizable* may be introduced as variant forms.

10. **veracity**

    The root of *veracity, verus,* true, appears in numerous words besides those listed on p. 341 of *Word Wealth* under –ver(it)–. *Verisimilitude* is an example.

# KEYS

**Setting-up Exercises**

1. ardently, benignly, celestially, civilly, complacently, credibly, culpably, eccentrically, futilely, incipiently, fallaciously, fluctuatingly, indolently, inferentially, (morally), retributively, temariously, veraciously.

3. Answers appear in notes on the individual words on pp. 99–101 of this manual.

**First Practice Set**

1. temerity, fallacy
2. ardent, fluctuations, inferences
3. indolence, complacent
4. incipient, retribution
5. benign, eccentric
6. celestial, morale
7. futile, subterfuge, utility
8. veracity, culpable
9. civil, credible

**Second Practice Set**

1. sloth, lethargy
2. supineness, somnolence
3. capricious, anomalous
4. effrontery, exculpate
5. quixotism, imposture
6. ruse, strategem
7. altruism, philanthropy
8. vacillation, esprit de corps
9. impudent, requital
10. alternation, idiosyncrasy

## Third Practice Set

1. c (indifferent)
2. b (discontented)
3. a (effectual)
4. e (normal)
5. c (terminal)
6. e (malevolent)
7. b (energetic)
8. a (untruthful)
9. a (laudable)
10. d (logical)

## The Right Word

**A.**
1. 9
2. 11
3. 6
4. 8
5. 10
6. 12
7. 3
8. 1
9. 4
10. 2

**B.**
1. 4
2. 10
3. 1
4. 6
5. 3
6. 8
7. 2
8. 12
9. 11
10. 7

## Bonus

1. civil, ineffectual
2. benefactions, fervent
3. morale, fluctuate
4. passionate, imply
5. maneuver, temerity

## Unit Test  *(Word Wealth Testing Program)*

1. d (arduous); m (indolent)
2. q (idiosyncrasy); h (eccentric)
3. g (celestial); a (credible)
4. i (ardent); b (effectual)
5. j (complacent); t (culprit)
6. k (credulous); bb (veracity)
7. v (fallacy); n (inference)
8. x (benignity); dd (altruism)
9. e (utilitarian); z (utility)
10. aa (ruse); u (stratagem)
11. s (quixotism); cc (retribution)
12. p (vacillation); y (effrontery); f (futile)

# unit nine

## FRENCH REVOLUTION

1. rancor  2. morose  3. vigilant  4. sanguine  5. belligerent
6. perversity  7. hypocrisy  8. gluttony  9. insidious  10. oblivion

## SEVEN SINISTER ADJECTIVES

1. **belligerent**

    The Latin roots are *bellum,* war, and *gerere,* to carry on. *Contentious* is a related word, applicable chiefly to verbal war.

2. **incorrigible**

    The positive form, *corrigible,* is less frequently used. *Corrigere,* the Latin root, with the sense of to lead straight, is also the root of *correct.* Thus an *incorrigible* person cannot be corrected or led straight. *Intractable* is a synonym. *Docile* and *manageable* are antonyms.

3. **morose**

    The Latin root, mor–, mos, simply means custom, habit, will. Antonyms are *genial, buoyant, sanguine. Acidulous* (mildly bitter or sour) is an additional related word.

4. **nefarious**

    The Latin root is *nefas,* crime, from ne–, not, plus fas, right, divine law. *Iniquitous* is an additional synonym. *Fiendish* and *diabolical* are slightly stronger words that could often be used in its place.

5. **pernicious**

    The Latin root *pernicies,* destruction, comes from per– plus nec–, nex, violent death. *Detrimental* is a mild synonym.

6. **venial**

    Antonyms are *mortal, deadly, inexcusable, unpardonable.*

7. **venomous**

The word comes from Latin *venim*, venom, assumed to be a variation of *venemum*, drug, poison, magic potion. It is a stronger word than *noxious* or even *deleterious*, partly because it sounds grimmer and partly because a snake's venom is deadly in certain cases.

## SIX KINDS OF EVIL

1. **depravity**

To make crooked is the literal meaning of the Latin root, *depravare*, from *pravus*, crooked, wrong, bad. The word denotes a state or condition rather than a single act.

2. **gluttony**

Like *glut*, it comes from the Latin verb *gluttire*, to swallow. *Ravenous* and *voracious* are synonyms of *gluttonous; gourmand* is a near synonym of *glutton*, and *ascetic* is more than an antonym. *Glutenous*, however, comes from *gluten*, a sticky ingredient of wheat flour.

3. **heresy**

The word comes from the Greek *hairesis*, choice, sect, from *hairein*, to take. *Unorthodox* is a synonym. *Apostasy* (abandoning what one believes) is usually a more inclusive word than *heresy*, but otherwise a fairly precise synonym. *Heresiarch* is one who founds a heresy.

4. **hypocrisy**

The Greek root, *hypokrisis*, means acting a part. The word implies deliberate falsification rather than simply feigning a virtue one does not have while endeavoring to attain it.

5. **perversity**

*Pervert* is now a familiar noun for a person who deviates from the natural, normal, moral ways of living.

6. **rancor**

*Animosity* is a good synonym, though more likely to be active, whereas *rancor* is a passive quality, stronger than *resentment*.

## SEVEN REMARKABLE ADJECTIVES

1. **intrepid**

The Latin root, in– plus *trepidus*, means not alarmed or anxious. Compare *trepidation* (alarm or dread) from the same root.

2. **laconic**

   *Prolix, verbose,* and *garrulous* are antonyms.

3. **militant**

   *Military, militarize, militarist,* and *militarism* fit in well here, being derivatives, like *militant*, of the Latin *miles, militis,* soldier.

4. **oblivious**

   The word comes ultimately from Latin *oblivisci,* to forget. *Abstraction, unconsciousness, slumber, concentration,* and *reverie* all make one oblivious for a few minutes or hours. *Unconscious* is thus a synonym. Note that *oblivion* is applied to a state of being forgotten as well as a state of unawareness of what is going on; but *oblivion* has a narrower spectrum of meaning than *oblivious.*

5. **sanguine**

   The noun forms, *sanguineness* and *sanguinity,* are seldom used. The related words provide additional antonyms for *morose* (p. 103 of this manual). *Sanguinary* has the literal meaning of bloody, and the noun form is *sanguinariness.*

6. **ubiquitous**

   The word is derived from Latin *ubique,* everywhere. *Pervasive* (spreading everywhere) is a partial synonym, except that it applies chiefly to odors, ideas, and attitudes and indicates a process while *ubiquitous* denotes a fact.

7. **vigilant**

   The word is derived from Latin *vigilare,* to keep awake. Antonyms include *unsuspecting, unwary,* and *heedless.*

# KEYS

## First Practice Set

**A**

1. depravity, nefarious
2. incorrigible, morose
3. rancor, belligerent
4. venomous, gluttony
5. oblivious, venial, pernicious, intrepid
6. heresy, sanguine
7. hypocritical, perversity
8. militant, laconic
9. vigilant, omnipresent

**B**

1. martial
2. splenetic
3. venial
4. ubiquitous
5. sanguine, exultant
6. obvious, oblivious
7. intrepidity
8. gluttony
9. chronic
10. vigilant, fractious

## Second Practice Set

1. wayward, refractory
2. venality, insidious
3. splenetic, polemical
4. sullen, surly
5. acrimonious, pestilential
6. rancid, venomous
7. atrocious, turpitude
8. martial, reprehensible
9. noxious, immorality
10. buoyant, exultant

## Third Practice Set

1. b (capable of reform)
2. d (good-natured)
3. c (benevolence)
4. c (aware)
5. d (wordy)
6. a (harmless)
7. e (timid)
8. b (inexcusable)
9. c (despairing)
10. b (unwary)

## UNIT TEST  (Word Wealth Testing Program)

1. v (perversity);  b (venial)
2. n (belligerent);  z (vigilance)
3. p (venomous);  y (hypocrisy); a (pernicious)
4. g (refractory);  h (incorrigible)
5. l (intrepid);  i (militant)
6. c (reprehensible);  q (sloth)
7. m (polemical);  k (acrimonious)
8. j (laconic);  o (splenetic)
9. s (malignity);  r (rancor)
10. d (oblivious);  w (heresy)
11. t (depravity);  x (turpitude)
12. u (gluttony);  f (deleterious)

# unit ten

## AMUSING

1. burlesque
2. ludicrousness
3. hilarity
4. cajolery
5. levity
6. facetiousness
7. satire
8. jocularity
9. repartee
10. bathos

## WORDS FOR RIDICULE

**1. derision**

*Risibility,* sensitiveness to the ridiculous, is often used in the plural.

**2. bathos**

Malapropisms (WW p. 239) often produce bathos: "Mrs. Prickle said she had a simply *pretentious* time at Mrs. Grubb's dinner party, but she had not *recuperated* yet." *Anticlimax* is a mild form of bathos, sometimes the same thing.

**3. burlesque**

The word comes, via French, from the Italian *burla,* a jest or takeoff.

**4. irony**

The word comes from the Greek word *eiron,* a dissembler in speech, from *eirein,* to speak. *Irony* has nothing to do with *iron* (the metal), which comes from Old English.

**5. satire**

The word is derived from Latin *satira, satura,* satiric poetry, poetic medley, from *(lanx) satura,* full plate, from *lanx,* plate, plus *satura,* full, sated, *i.e.,* plate filled with various fruits; a mixture; a medley. The Romans accepted this derivation because their satires, with some influence from the Greek, were of such infinite variety.

## WORDS FOR LIGHT-HEARTED USES

1. **levity**

    *Flippancy* is a synonym, but with the difference indicated in the comments under this entry word in the text. *Buoyant gaiety* is another, but not the boisterous gaiety that characterizes hilarity.

2. **facetiousness**

    The word comes from the Latin adjective *facetus*, elegantly witty. *Facetiae*, the Latin plural of *facetia*, a jest, is rarely used.

3. **flippancy**

    The word appears to be to some degree a modern invention, which partly defines itself by sound. *Flip*, meaning saucy or impertinent, is a rootless word still considered colloquial.

4. **hilarity**

    *Hilarity* is high-spirited, but it comes from a very similar Greek word, *hilaros*, meaning merely cheerful. The name *Hilary* comes from this root, but *Hilda* and *Hildebrand* are derived from a Germanic root for battle or war.

5. **jocularity**

    *Jocularity* is good-natured and sportive but not witty, boisterous, disrespectful, or imaginative, even though the word is descended from the Latin *jocus*, a joke or jest.

6. **ludicrousness**

    This is an inclusive word applying chiefly to actions and situations. The Latin root *ludus*, a play or game causing laughter, undergirds this usage.

7. **repartee**

    From the French word *repartir*, to retort, this word has earlier roots in Middle French.

## ADJECTIVES

1. **bohemian**

    Bohemia got its reputation when it was a part of Austria-Hungary before World War I, but it reportedly still has many gypsies.

2. **catatonic**

   *Catatonia* is one of several schizophrenic syndromes or patterns.

3. **ecumenical**

   The Greek root *oikoumenikos,* of or from the entire world, comes in turn from a Greek word for house, *oikos.*

4. **empirical**

   The word has nothing to do with empires but comes from the Greek word *peira,* an experiment. *Empire,* on the other hand, comes from the Latin noun *imperium,* which became *empire* in Old French and subsequently in English.

5. **nether**

   *Nethermost, netherward,* and *netherworld* may be mentioned.

6. **palatable**

   *Edible* means simply fit to eat, and *potable* fit to drink. *Viable* means able to stay alive and develop. *Savory* is a synonym, but *succulent* (juicy) has a sophomoric quality. The best antonym of *palatable* is *unpalatable.*

7. **paranoid**

   The Greek root is *para–,* beside or contrary, plus *nous,* mind.

8. **psychedelic**

   A new word, *psychedelic* was created in a 1966 *Atlantic Monthly* article to describe the kind of experiences provided by LSD and other hallucinogens. (*Delic* comes from the Greek verb *delein,* to make manifest.) It has proved viable, probably because no other suitable word was available.

# KEYS

**First Practice Set***

1. bathos, hilarity
2. burlesque, ludicrousness
3. repartee, palatable
4. jovial, facetiousness
5. satire, derision
6. flippancy, bohemianism
7. levity, nether
8. catatonic, empirical
9. psychedelic, paranoiac
10. ecumenical, ironic
11. ludicrous, repartee
12. flippant, levity
13. jocularly
14. burlesque, derision
15. ironic, bohemian
16. empirical
17. facetiousness, nether
18. paranoid, palatable

*Inform your students that, in this First Practice Set, a number of the entry words are used more than once.

## Second Practice Set

1. catalepsy, jocose
2. jovial, parody
3. pun, spoonerism
4. jocular, catalyst
5. caricature, realistically
6. jocund, mirth
7. levitation, levigation
8. catatonia, cataclysm
9. catacombs, cataract
10. travesty, sarcasm

## Third Practice Set

|   | | Matching Verbs | Matching Adjectives |
|---|---|---|---|
| 1. | c (levity) | 1. 5 | 1. 11 |
| 2. | a (hilarity) | 2. 7 | 2. 12 |
| 3. | b (jocular) | 3. 10 | 3. 9 |
| 4. | d (gravitation) | 4. 1 | 4. 7 |
| 5. | b (distasteful) | 5. 8 | 5. 2 |
| 6. | d (pernicious) | 6. 2 | 6. 5 |
| 7. | d (grandeur) | 7. 4 | 7. 3 |
| 8. | d (sectarianism) | 8. 11 | 8. 4 |
| 9. | b (lugubriousness) | 9. 6 | 9. 1 |
| 10. | d (flippancy) | 10. 9 | 10. 6 |

## Extra

2. In Part I Swift is satirizing the absurd exertions people undertake for political preferment; the petty jealousies persons of genius encounter when their actions deprive others of the glory they hoped to attain; and the needless complexities of the law. He satirizes many other follies incidentally, like parents' excessive or sentimental fondness for their children.

   Part II ridicules in a more distant and general way the evils of the English political system of that day as Swift saw it and the way one person who has power will exploit another person for profit.

   Part III satirizes English political domination of Ireland (the flying island); the absurdity of wanting to live too long (Struldbrugs); the absentmindedness of thinkers, scholars, and political figures (Grand Academy of Lagado); ridiculous projects in scientific investigation; the unreliability of historical accounts and traditions (Glubbdubdriv); and numerous other follies.

   In Part IV Swift satirizes human greed, emphasis on sex, simian behavior, and other vices through the Yahoos. Beasts in the shape of humans, the Yahoos are contrasted with the Houyhnhnms, horses endowed with reason. The simplicity and virtues of the latter point up the disgusting brutality of the Yahoos. Swift's purpose in Part IV is to make pride and vanity absurd by stressing the animal nature of human beings.

4. Derisively, bathetically, burlesquely, ironically, satirically, facetiously, flippantly, hilariously, jocularly, ludicrously, catatonically, ecumenically, empirically, palatably, paranoidally, psychedelically. (No adverbs are formed from the following entry words: *levity, repartee, bohemian, nether.*)

5. The hard palate (Latin *palatum*) is involved in pronunciation as well as, ostensibly, in savoring food. The latter function is, then, the springboard to the idea of mental relish and intellectual taste.

**Ten Defiant Adjectives**

Suggested student assignment: Be a promoter of word revival. Some of the adjectives in this list are useful because no other word readily replaces them. Which ones are they? Write sentences using them. Find ways to employ them in everyday situations.

## Unit Test   *(Word Wealth Testing Program)*

1.  f (ludicrous);   r (levity)
2.  aa (travesty);   c (bohemian);   l (derisive)
3.  z (spoonerism);   o (hilarity)
4.  a (ironic);   i (bathetic)
5.  u (burlesque);   m (satiric)
6.  q (pun);   d (jocular)
7.  j (flippant);   y (repartee)
8.  bb (catatonia);   p (facetiousness)
9.  e (palatable);   b (empirical)
10. k (psychedelic);   v (hallucinogen)
11. g (ecumenical);   x (paranoia)
12. s (parody);   h (jocund)

# part three

## unit one

### SOMETIMES

1. collaborate  2. condone  3. deter  4. dilemma  5. calumny
6. consternation  7. alacrity  8. coincide  9. construe  10. emanate

### VERBS OF ATTITUDE AND SOCIAL RELATIONSHIP

1. **cavil**

   The Latin root, *cavillari*, means to banter or jest. The agent form is *caviler* or *caviller*.

2. **coincide**

   This is a good place to discuss briefly the use of coincidence in fiction, which may be used to get the characters into trouble but is frowned upon when used to extricate them. Introduce *juxtaposition, juxtapose* (to place two things next to each other, usually for comparison).

3. **collaborate**

   Other –labor– words include *laborious, laboratory, elaborate,* and variant forms. See also p. 287 of *Word Wealth* under *con–...syn–*.

4. **condone**

   *Indulgence* also excuses questionable behavior. The Latin root of *condone* is *donare*, to give, with the sense of to go along with. *Donate, donation, donor, donee* come from the same root (WW p. 351). *Done*, from Old English, is akin to Old High German *tuon*, to do.

5. **construe**

   *Construct* comes from the same Latin verb, *struere*, to pile or build.

6. **contemplate**

   The root is the Latin word *templum*, temple, and thus the word connotes a quiet place conducive to reflection (see *meditate*, WW p. 11).

### 7. deter

The Latin root is *terrere,* to frighten, from which come *terror* and its five variant forms, but not the *terra–* (earth) words (WW p. 359).

### 8. disparage

Like *peer* and *par, disparage* comes from the Latin word *par,* an equal.

### 9. emanate

Derived from Latin *manare,* to flow, the word is used extensively in reference to light, radio waves, or radiation and thus any forces or influences that fly through space. *Radiate* is a synonym, with narrower and more material uses centering in images of light, heat, and electromagnetic vibrations. Compare *extravasate* (flow forth slowly).

### 10. exemplify

Add *exemplar* (a pattern or person worthy of imitation). *Exemplum,* taken over from the Latin word meaning example, is a medieval term for a moralized story or anecdote. Chaucer includes several in the *Canterbury Tales*.

## SITUATIONS AND RESPONSES

### 1. alacrity

The word is derived from Latin *alacer,* lively. The adjective *alacritous* is occasionally used.

### 2. calumny

Calumny comes from Latin *calumnia,* from *calvi,* to deceive. *Calumniator* is the person or agent word. A pupil might look up *pasquinade* (a lampoon, especially one posted in a public place). The word comes from a statue of Pasquino in Rome on which lampoons were often posted.

### 3. chagrin

*Shagreen,* pronounced as spelled, is a kind of rough-surfaced rawhide from the skin of a horse, camel, or shark.

### 4. consternation

The root is the Latin *sternare,* to stare. *Trepidation* connotes trembling, *palpitation,* a throbbing of the heart. *Perturbation* (a state of agitation) was once used to mean an apparent irregularity or disturbance in the motion of heavenly bodies.

5. **dilemma**

The word can be traced to Greek *dilemmatos*, involving two assumptions, from *lemma*, assumption. *Dubiety* is a state of doubt or uncertainty less disturbing than a *quandary*. *Incertitude* (a state of uncertainty) may be mentioned also.

6. **enigma**

Spelled *aenigma* in Latin, the word derived ultimately from Greek *ainissesthai*, to speak in riddles, from *ainos*, fable. For Joseph Conrad, Lord Jim "seemed to stand at the heart of a vast enigma."

7. **erudition**

*Savant*, from the French verb *savoir* and the Latin verb *sapere*, connotes great knowledge and wisdom. *Pundit*, from Sanskrit, connotes extensive learning only and may be used humorously.

8. **fecundity**

Joseph Conrad used the word in one form or another several times in *Lord Jim*. In Chapter 35, for example, he speaks (through Marlow) of "the primeval smell of fecund earth."

9. **immolation**

The Latin root is *mola*, meal, from the custom of sprinkling meal on a sacrificial victim before killing it. Im– = in– meaning on.

10. **innovation**

Other nov– words are listed under –nov– (WW p. 348) including *novice, novelty, novitiate*. One may also list *renovate, nova, Novocain*.

# KEYS

### First Practice Set

1. dilemma, collaborate
2. innovation, condone
3. calumnies, disparage
4. chagrin, deter
5. construe, erudition
6. consternation, contemplate
7. cavil, immolation
8. alacrity, enigma
9. emanate, exemplify
10. fecundity, coincides

### Second Practice Set

1. impasse, quandary
2. depreciate, minimize
3. verve, vivacity
4. emerge, animation
5. inception, genesis
6. absolution, exoneration
7. lampoon, issue
8. scurrility, libel
9. cryptogram, embarkation
10. dissuade, intimidate

## Third Practice Set

1. b (alacrity—initiative)
2. d (collaborate—coincide)
3. b (dilemma—deterred)
4. c (disparage—emanate)
5. a (calumnies—exemplify)
6. b (cryptogram—collaboration)
7. d (cavil—construe)
8. a (condone—chagrin)
9. d (an enigma—consternation)
10. c (contemplation—erudition)

## The Right Word

1. collaborator, verve
2. inception, quandary
3. disparagement, abash
4. exemplary, calumny
5. emanate, genesis

## Exercises

1. These include *vivid, vivify, vivification, viviparity, viviparous* (bringing forth live offspring rather than eggs, as in oviparous reproduction), *vivisect, vivisection, vivisectionist*. Prefixes in IV, 1 and IV, 2 give *revive, revival, revivify, revivification, convivial, conviviality*.

2. *Hypo-* words worth knowing include *hypocrite, hypodermic* (under the skin), *hypogenous* (growing on the under surface of something), *hypoglycemia* (deficiency of blood sugar), *hyypostasis* (settling of blood in the lower part of the body), *hypotenuse, hypothecate* (pledge property to another as security for a debt), *hypothermia* (a body temperature below normal), *hypothesis* (WW pp. 38, 69), *hypothesize, hypothetical,* and *hypothyroid (ism)*.

## Unit Test  (*Word Wealth Testing Program*)

1. y (cavil); o (dilemma)
2. b (collaboration); e (collusion)
3. a (coincidence); x (deter)
4. k (erudition); c (fecundity)
5. p (sophistication); r (exemplify)
6. bb (condone); w (minimize)
7. cc (depreciate); z (deride)
8. i (enigma); n (chagrin)
9. u (emerge); s (emanate)
10. q (disparage); f (irreverence)
11. d (quandary); m (impasse)
12. h (alacrity); j (vivacity); v (detract)

# unit two

## COUPLES

1. emancipate    2. reconcile    3. mediate    4. reciprocate    5. temporize
6. vindicate    7. relegate    8. placate    9. repudiate    10. felicitate

## ADJECTIVES

1. **altruistic**

    From French *altruisme*, from *autrui*, other people, the word derives ultimately from Latin *alter*, other. Note that although *beneficent* and *benevolent* are sometimes used interchangeably, *beneficent* connotes good deeds and *benevolent* merely attitudes or gestures of well-wishing.

2. **astute**

    The word has its origin in Latin *astus*, cunning. *Astuteness* stresses insight and a capacity to act accordingly. Among the related words, *discerning* means that one sees clearly what is happening. An *adroit* person acts cleverly and commendably, but *wily* actions are by implication crafty and evasive. A *sagacious* person is wise as well as shrewd, and a *perspicacious* person penetrates the complexities of life more deeply than a *discerning* person.

3. **authentic**

    The word comes through Old French and Latin from Greek *authentes*, the doer of a deed. Compare *bona fide*, which applies primarily to a situation in which honesty or good faith is involved rather than the genuineness of an object or of information. *Veritable* means genuine or readily demonstrable, but is used chiefly in an intensive way for literary effect, as in the expression, "proverbs are a *veritable* gold mine of wise sayings."

4. **cumulative**

    The word can be traced to Latin *cumulare*, to heap up, from *cumulus*, a heap. Job's sufferings were *cumulative*. Compound interest is *cumulative*.

5. **despondent**

    Bring in other –spond– (promise) words and their variants, especially *respond* and *correspond*.

## 6. didactic

The word derives from Greek *didaskein,* to teach. Introduce the noun form in such phrases as "Emerson's *didacticism."* One might discuss didacticism in literature, whether literature should be didactic in intention (if not explicitly expressed), etc.

## 7. ecclesiastical

The word is of Greek origin, from *ekklesia,* assembly, from *kalein,* to call. The *ecclesia* was the assembly of people who had been summoned. Only free citizens were called, however, not slaves. Mention *liturgical, ecumenical, hierarchical,* and perhaps other words used often in connection with churches.

## 8. felicitous

The Latin root is *felicitas,* from *felix,* happy, hence the name Felix, once a dignified Roman name, and its feminine form Felicia. *Feline* comes from a different root.

## 9. imperial

*Empire* comes from the same root as *imperial.* The title *imperator,* another form of the same word, was given to successful Roman generals and later to emperors.

## 10. odious

*Intolerant* is an additional "hate" word. *Odium* is a state of being hated, but *odeum* is a Greek-derived term for a small theater. *Ode* comes from the Greek word *oide,* song.

# VERBS

## 1. emancipate

*Manciple* (steward) comes from the same Latin root, *manceps,* purchaser, derived from *manus,* hand, plus *capere,* to take.

## 2. mediate

*Mediate,* meaning middle or in between, may be added. Other "middle" words include *medieval, mediocre, Mediterranean, medium, median*—but not *medicine, medullated,* or *medlar* (a kind of Eurasian tree).

3. **reciprocate**

    A *reciprocal* pronoun, such as *one another* or *each other*, denotes mutual action or cross relationship between the parties of a plural subject. *Recidivist* (habitual criminal, one who relapses) is a related word, with *recidivism* as the noun form.

4. **reconcile**

    The word comes from Latin *conciliare*, to conciliate. *Reconcilability*, *reconcilement*, and *reconciliatory* are variant forms occasionally used.

5. **relegate**

    *Relegate* derives ultimately from Latin *legare*, to depute, send an emissary, from *lex*, law. *Assign*, *consign*, and *commit* are related words. Only *commit* (as to an institution) has the implication of getting rid of or to some degree consigning to oblivion as does *relegate*. *Commit* is used typically of persons, *relegate* more often of objects.

6. **repudiate**

    *Disclaim*, *discredit*, *abrogate*, and *annul* are related words, each with its own special use (see *abrogate*, WW p. 256).

7. **subsidize**

    *Subsidize* is another of the numerous words from the Latin verb *sedere*, to sit. To *subsidize* something is thus to sit under it and uphold it.

8. **temporize**

    This is one of the "time" words from *tempus*, time, along with *temporal*, *temporary*, *tempo*, and *temper* (to moderate or soften).

9. **usurp**

    The root meaning from the Latin is to take or seize (*rapere*) by use (*usu*). *Rapacity* (WW p. 249) is a projection of *rapere*. Other "use" words (from Latin *usus*) include *usual*, *usufruct* (legal right to use something belonging to another), *usury*. *Utensil* and *utility* belong to the same family.

10. **vindicate**

    The word comes from Latin *vindicare*, to lay claim to, avenge, from *vindex*, claimant, avenger. *Confirm* and *substantiate* are synonyms. *Exonerate* (WW p. 124) and *exculpate* are related words of similar meaning.

# KEYS

## First Practice Set

1. ecclesiastical, felicitous
2. astute, emancipate
3. authentic, vindicate
4. relegate, reconcile
5. altruistic, mediate
6. temporize, usurp
7. subsidize, despondent
8. imperial, odious
9. cumulative, repudiate
10. didactic, reciprocate

## Second Practice Set

1. intercessor, intermediary
2. placate, arbitrate
3. temporal, arrogate
4. historicity, charismatic
5. philanthropist, humanitarian
6. dissent, redeem
7. disenthralls, disencumbers
8. extemporaneous, acumen
9. feudal, regal
10. patriarchal, impudent

## Third Practice Set

1. c (pacify:reconcile)
2. a (vindicate:incriminate)
3. b (unselfish:altruistic)
4. d (usurper:inheritor)
5. c (extemporaneous: premeditated)
6. b (cremate:corpse)
7. c (reputation:vindicate)
8. c (emancipate:enthrall)
9. d (humanitarian:altruism)
10. a (slavery:emancipation)

## Unit Test  *(Word Wealth Testing Program)*

1. x (mediate);  bb (reconcile)
2. q (intercede);  e (despondent)
3. o (vindicate);  cc (authenticate)
4. a (cumulative);  u (relegate)
5. i (monarchial);  d (temporal)
6. z (usurp);  l (temporary)
7. m (extemporaneous);  s (repudiate)
8. g (astute);  p (temporize)
9. j (charismatic);  b (patriarchal);  n (imperial)
10. t (compile);  c (ecclesiastical)
11. r (placate);  h (odious)
12. v (emancipate);  y (disenthrall)

# unit three

## OPPOSITES

1. perspicacity  2. succinctness  3. tentativeness  4. prostration
5. vicissitude   6. sagacity      7. surfeit        8. propriety
9. recumbency   10. propensity

## NOUNS

1. **perspicacity**

   Note that *conspicuous, despicable, suspicious,* and their variants are also formed from the root –spic– (WW p. 342).

2. **predilection**

   The root *diligere,* to prefer, is also the root of *diligent,* which root comes in turn from *legere,* to select. Thus *legend, legion, eligible,* and *elite* all derive from the one root, *legere. Legate, legation,* and *delegate* come from *legare,* to send, however.

3. **prerogative**

   The root *rogare,* to ask, is the familiar root of *interrogate, arrogate, derogate,* and *rogation,* but not of *rogue.*

4. **propensity**

   This is one of the words from –pend–, –pense–, presented in *Word Wealth* on p. 289.

5. **propriety**

   *Proprietor, proprietary, proper,* and *property* also come from the same root, the Latin noun *proprietas,* property, and thence from *proprius,* one's own.

6. **prostration**

   *Stratum* and *strata* come from the same root, *sternere,* to spread out, but not *demonstration, consternation,* or *stern.*

### 7. restitution

Compare *destitution, constitution, institution,* and other words from *statuere,* to set up. *Statue* and *statute* are also derivatives.

### 8. sagacity

*Saga* is a Norse word, and *sagamore* has an Indian origin.

### 9. surfeit

The literal meaning is to overdo something, from the Latin *sur-,* over, and *facere,* to make or do. The word came via Medieval French, which changed the spelling. *Counterfeit* and *forfeit* gained their meanings and spellings in the same way.

### 10. vicissitude

*Fluctuations* are less dramatic, less extreme, less poetic, and more properly applied to changing quantities or forces than *vicissitudes,* which is used chiefly of one's fortunes. *Mutability* is changeability, especially of fortunes or fates. *Week* comes ultimately from the same Latin root as *vicissitude, vicis,* change, but it comes by way of Old English. *Vicissitudinous* is sometimes used.

# ADJECTIVES

### 1. lambent

The Latin root is *lambere,* to lick. *Lamb* is an unrelated word of Old English origin.

### 2. latent

The Latin root is *latere,* to lie hidden. *Elated* and *elation* come not from *latere,* but from the verb *efferre,* to carry out or away. *Quiescent* and *abeyant* (lapsed or discontinued) may also be added to the related words.

### 3. marital

The Latin root is *maritus,* husband, married, and is not to be confused with –mari– (sea) words, which include *marinated* (steeped in brine, especially a meat or fish). –Mari–, –marine– is presented in *Word Wealth* on p. 333.

### 4. partisan

From the Latin word *pars,* part, *partisan* owes its ending to the French spelling which it retains. *Bipartisan* may be mentioned, also *nonpartisan.*

5. **recumbent**

   The root is *cumbere*, to lie down. *Incubus* (nightmare), *incubate*, *succubus* (a vicious demon), and *succumb* are traced to the Latin verb *cubare*, to lie (in, upon) or, as in *succubus* and *succumb*, to lie (under).

6. **salient**

   The root of the word is Latin *salire*, to leap. Synonyms include *noticeable*, *remarkable*, *outstanding*, *signal* (outstanding, significant), *striking*.

7. **seditious**

   *Sedition* does not share its root, *itio*, act of going, with *condition* (the root of which is *dicere*, to say), with *rendition*, with *edition* (from *edere*, to bring forth), with *fruition*, or with *inanition*.

8. **succinct**

   The root *cingere*, to bind, links *succinct* with *precinct*, *cinch*, and *cincture* (girdle). Note that *cinque* (five), *cingquain*, *cinquefoil* (design having five joined foils) come from the Latin word *quinque*, five.

9. **tangible**

   It is one of the "touch" words from –tang–, –tact–, several of which are presented in *Word Wealth* on p. 342.

10. **tentative**

    The root *tentare*, to feel or try, appears in *tempt*, *tentacle*, and *attempt*, but not in *tent*, *intent*, *content*, or *contempt*.

# KEYS

**First Practice Set**

1. predilection, perspicacity
2. propensity, prostration
3. restitution, vicissitudes
4. tentative, propriety
5. prerogative, latent
6. sagacity, surfeit
7. lambent, recumbent
8. tangible, succinct
9. salient, sedition, seized wrongfully
10. partisan, marital

**Second Practice Set**

1. predisposition, bias
2. penchant, proclivity
3. reinstatement, conjugal
4. disciple, devotee
5. dormant, discernible
6. advocate, potential
7. incumbent, compensation
8. manifest, subversion
9. recuperation, domestic
10. palpable, reparation

**Third Practice Set**

1. d (obtuseness:perspicacity)
2. a (perspicacity:sagacity)
3. a (salience:inconspicuousness)
4. c (imperceptible:discernible)
5. c (palpable:tangible)
6. b (predisposition:proclivity)
7. d (seditious:treason)
8. a (candidate:incumbent)
9. c (invariability:vicissitude)
10. b (perspicacity:stupidity)

## Unit Test  *(Word Wealth Testing Program)*

1. o (vicissitude);  u (sagacity); e (tentative)
2. s (prerogative); x (predilection)
3. f (partisan);  m (perspicacity); z (bias)
4. q (compensation);  n (reparation); aa (restitution)
5. bb (subversion);  t (treason)
6. i (salient);  a (marital)
7. p (reinstatement); v (rehabilitation)
8. k (perceptible);  b (palpable); l (manifest)
9. r (surfeit);  j (garrulous); c (incumbent)
10. w (proclivity);  y (ellipses)

# unit four

## WEIRD OR SINISTER

1. a (occultism)
2. b (a coalition)
3. c (plagiarism)
4. c (chimerical)
5. c (exotic)
6. c (aesthetic)
7. a (relevant)
8. c (a fetish)
9. d (portentous)
10. b (ineffable)

## NOUNS

1. **coalition**

   The word is derived from Latin *alescere,* to grow. A *federation* or a *confederation* is a loose but lasting kind of alliance in which the members sacrifice relatively little in identity or independence. A *league* is likely to be a unified organization, for a time, at least, but it may be an alliance of elements, entities, or political bodies which retain freedom of action.

2. **covenant**

   The word comes, like *convene,* from the Latin verb *convenire.* The Solemn League and Covenant was an agreement between the parliaments of England and Scotland in 1643 to establish and extend Presbyterianism in England. A *Convenanter* was a person who supported this Covenant or an earlier Scottish Presbyterian Covenant in 1638.

3. **fetish**

   It is one of the less obvious derivatives of the Latin verb *facere,* to make (see –fact–, –fect–, –fict–, WW p. 288), but its more immediate source is French. It is sometimes spelled *fetich,* and the person form *fetishist* is used.

4. **incentive**

   The root is the Latin verb *canere,* to sing. Thus the word suggests that which makes one sing. *Motivation* is the more technical word used by psychologists and educators.

5. **incubus**

   See notes on *recumbent* on p. 123 of this manual.

## 6. insurrection

As an *insurrection* is a rising up *against* (in-) something established, so a *resurrection* is a rising up *again* (re-) from a literal or figurative death.

## 7. paradox

Compare *orthodox* (right teaching) and *heterodox* (other than right teaching). *Paradox* is contrary (*i.e.*, contradictory) teaching (see –doc–, –doctrin–, –dox, WW p. 339; para– WW p. 330).

## 8. paragon

The root meaning is against (Greek, para–) a whetstone (*akone*). Thus *paragon* is not related to *octagon, pentagon,* or *polygon*. Its root is *parakonan,* to whet, and the word connotes the emotional effect and mind-sharpening value of paradoxes.

## 9. plagiarism

*Plagiaristic* and *plagiary* are occasionally used.

## 10. solstice

The root verb, *sistere,* to stand, is the familiar root of *insist, consist, persist, resist,* and dozens of other English words.

# ADJECTIVES

## 1. aesthetic

The root of *aesthetic* is Greek *aisthanesthai,* to perceive. *Anaesthetic* is merely a negative form of this word. Compare *kinesthetic,* pertaining to the sense of feeling or movement, position, or motion, especially muscular; it is also spelled *kinaesthetic*.

## 2. chimerical

*Incubus* and *succubus* (under *recumbent* on p. 123 of this manual) suggest horror and terror to a greater degree than chimerical.

## 3. exotic

The word comes from the Greek word *exo,* outside. Compare *exoteric* (intended for the outside world rather than a chosen few), a word which comes from the comparative form of *exo* in Greek. *Exoteric* is thus the opposite of *esoteric,* which means restricted to the few.

4. **forensic**

   The suffix –ensis–, to which –ic is added, appears also in other words, including *amanuensis* (secretary).

5. **ineffable**

   Like *inert, inane, incessant, incognito, incorrigible, inexorable, inferior, insidious, ineffable* belongs to a fairly large group of words which have only a negative form. This fact thus stirred David M. Crothers to start his crusade to restore their lost positive forms, *ert, ane, cessant, cognito,* etc. The positive root of *ineffable* is Latin *effari,* to speak out, from *fari,* to speak.

6. **maudlin**

   The word is derived from Old French *Maudelene* or *Madeleine* from (Mary) *Magdalen,* often depicted as a weeping penitent. The name of Magdalen College in Oxford is pronounced like *maudlin. Fatuous* (WW p. 220) is a related word for one who is complacently silly or sentimental.

7. **occult**

   The word is not related to *cult, culture,* or *cultivate* but comes from the Latin verb *occulere,* to cover over. *Occultation* in astronomy is the eclipse (covering over) of one heavenly body by another.

8. **portentous**

   The Latin root is *portendere,* to stretch forth (see –tend– WW p. 309).

9. **relevant**

   The word comes from the same Latin root as *relieve,* which is the verb *relevare,* to lift up again and thus intellectually to bear upon (the topic under discussion).

10. **sadistic**

    *Masochistic* is an adjective indicating the sense of release or pleasure that sadists feel in making their victims suffer.

# KEYS

**First Practice Set**

1. covenant, relevant
2. coalition, incubus
3. forensic, insurrection
4. chimerical, ineffable
5. exotic, occult
6. paradox, portentous
7. sadistic, paragon
8. solstice, plagiarize
9. maudlin, incentive
10. aesthetic, fetish

## Second Practice Set
1. apposite, quixotic
2. talisman, amulet
3. insurgent, riot
4. uprising, boycott
5. hydra, compact
6. diabolism, chimera
7. bibliolatry, idolatry
8. heliolatry, zoolatry
9. apropos, pertinent
10. exorcism, germane

## Third Practice Set
1. d (plagiarism:originality)
2. d (covenant:contract)
3. d (visionary:quixotic)
4. b (earthly:ineffable)
5. a (hydra:chimera)
6. c (orator:forensics)
7. d (insurrection:revolution)
8. a (fanciful:chimerical)
9. a (necromancy:diabolism)
10. d (sun bathing:heliolatry)

## The Right Word
1. portend
2. paradox
3. insurgent
4. plagiarism
5. quixotic
6. exotic
7. aesthete
8. covenant/compact
9. irrelevant
10. chimerical

## Queries
1. Worship words:
   hagiolatry—worship of saints
   iconolatry—worship of images
   necrolatry—worship of (or excessive reverence for) the dead
   anthropolatry—worship of man
   matriolatry—worship of mothers

   One may add *gyneolatry,* worship of women; *heliolatry,* worship of the sun; and *bibliolatry,* worship of books. *Marxolatry* would be the worship of Karl Marx; and *geneolatry* would be the worship of family or excessive pride in one's ancestors. *Criminolatry* would be excessive admiration for criminals, and *astrolatry* worship of the stars.

2. coalitional, covenantal, fetishistic, insurrectional (insurrectionary), paradoxical, plagiaristic, solstitial. *Incentive* may be used as either an adjective or a noun.

   **Activity:** In the Adjectives section of the unit, have students list the noun form of the word as represented in the example sentences.

## Unit Test   *(Word Wealth Testing Program)*
1. p (insurrection);  t (coalition)
2. j (exotic);  cc (fetishism);  x (heliolatry)
3. m (necromancy);  z (occultism)
4. aa (mutiny);  r (solstice)
5. c (forensic);  v (incentive)
6. l (relevant);  o (chimera)
7. w (hydra);  n (incubus)
8. y (paradox);  g (portentous)
9. e (sadistic);  a (aesthetic)
10. q (paragon);  i (germane)
11. s (dilettante);  b (ineffable)
12. d (maudlin);  f (recondite)

# unit five

## FAMILY GATHERING

1. b (quiet)
2. c (haughty)
3. b (very discriminating)
4. d (frank)
5. b (spirited)
6. d (fatuous)
7. a (ostentatious)
8. d (gregarious)
9. a (captious)
10. c (dogmatic)

## BEHAVIORISTICS

1. **aggressive**

   *Aggressor* is widely used, especially of nations, and *nonaggression* pacts are a familiar diplomatic activity.

2. **arrogant**

   *Arrogant* is one of the many ramifications of the Latin verb *rogare*, to ask. See note under *prerogative* on p. 121 of this manual and –rog– with notes (WW p. 306).

3. **captious**

   One of the more elusive derivatives of the Latin verb *capere*, to take, *captious* implies that one is too "taken" by the "fun" of being excessively critical. *Captive* and its variants come from this root.

4. **cynical**

   *Cynical* comes from the Greek word *kynikos*, like a dog—obviously not a friendly one. Compare *hound*, which has been traced to the same root, in much the same way that *hundred* is derived from the Latin word *centum*, *i.e.*, by the operation of Grimm's law.

5. **dogmatic**

   The –dog–, like the –dox– in *orthodox*, comes from the Greek root *dokein*, to believe. See note under *paradox* on p. 126 of this manual.

6. **fastidious**

   The Latin root, *fastus*, disdain or contempt, is not the root of *fast* or *steadfast*. Compare *captious*, above, which implies a fondness for finding fault rather than the sincere sense of superiority which underlies *fastidiousness*.

## 7. fatuous

This word comes from the Latin word *fatuus*, foolish. *Ignis fatuus*, foolish or fool's fire, is the Latin term for the glow sometimes seen over a swamp at night and poetically called by the old Scandinavian phrase *will-o'-the-wisp*.

## 8. garrulous

The Latin root *garrire* means to chatter or prattle.

## 9. gregarious

See –greg– (WW p. 316).

## 10. impetuous

*Impetus* (incentive, momentum) comes from the same root, *petere*, to rush at; so do *petulant* and *propitiate*.

## 11. ingenuous

Both *ingenious* and *ingenuous* derive from the same Latin root *gignere*, to produce, the former by way of the Latin noun *ingenium*, inborn attribute, the latter by way of the adjective *ingenuus*, inborn or freeborn.

## 12. nostalgic

The suffix –algia comes from the Greek word *algein*, to feel pain. Compare *neuralgia*.

## 13. ostentatious

Along with *ostensible* and the variants of both, this word belongs to the progeny of the Latin verb *tendere*, to stretch, os– being a variation of ob(s), against. Thus comes the hint of flaunting something, a hint which is implicit in both *ostentatious* and *ostensible*.

## 14. sinuous

Compare *sinusitis*, inflammation of the sinuses (curved, air-filled cavities in the skull). *Sinuosity* is sometimes used instead of *sinuousness*. The Latin root, *sinus*, bend or curve, is also the root of *insinuate*.

## 15. taciturn

The Latin verb *tacere*, to be silent, is the root word of *reticent* as it is of *tacit* and *taciturn*. The –tact– words (WW p. 342), however, come not from *tacere* but from *tangere*, to touch.

16. **truculent**

    The word comes from the Latin adjective *trux, trucis,* fierce or savage, and is *not* the source of *truce, truck, truant, truckle,* or *obtrusive.*

17. **unctuous**

    The Roman Catholic rite of Extreme Unction may well be mentioned; it is the act of anointing administered by the priest to a person who is dying.

18. **valid**

    The root of *valid* is the Latin verb *valere,* to be strong. *Evaluate* and the other "value" words come from the same root.

19. **versatile**

    In addition to all the –vert–, –vers–, –verge– words listed or indicated on p. 299 of *Word Wealth,* the following may be listed: *versant, versicle* (a short or little verse), *versicolor* (iridescent), *versify, verso* (back of a coin or leaf of a manuscript), *vertebra,* and *vertex.*

20. **volatile**

    Other –vol– words, from *volare,* to fly, include *volant* (flying or nimble), *volary* (aviary), *volitant* (flying or able to fly), and *volitation* (act of flying), but not, of course, *volition* or *volcano. Volatilize, volatizable,* and *volatilization* are familiar variants of *volatile,* especially in technology.

# KEYS

## If Time Permits

1. aggressively, arrogantly, captiously, cynically, dogmatically, fastidiously, fatuously, garrulously, gregariously, impetuously, ingenuously, nostalgically, ostentatiously, sinuously, taciturnly, truculently, unctuously, validly, versatilely, volatilely.

2. forwardness, officiousness, assertiveness, presumptuousness, disdainfulness, insolence, superciliousness, peevishness, petulance, contentiousness, querulousness, hypercriticism, satire, sarcasm, sardonicism, pessimism, misanthropy, particularity, squeamishness, scrupulousness, prudishness, foolishness, oafishness, asininity, impulsiveness, precipitancy, precipitousness, ingenuousness, ingenuity, disingenuousness, candor, nostalgia, garishness, undulation, circuitousness, tacitness, reticence, valor, invalidity, invalidation, volatility, stability, bovinity.

## First Practice Set

1. taciturn, garrulous
2. arrogant, nostalgic
3. aggressive, valid
4. versatile, captious
5. unctuous, truculent
6. fatuous, impetuous
7. volatile, gregarious
8. ingenuous, fastidious
9. sinuous, dogmatic
10. ostentatious, cynical

## Second Practice Set

1. näive, infatuation
2. reticent, scrupulous
3. sarcastic, contentious
4. fluency, glibness
5. hypercritical, querulous
6. circuitous, undulating
7. serpentine, effusive
8. impulsive, valiant
9. prudishness, satirical
10. misanthropy, sardonic

## Third Practice Set

1. b (loquacious:garrulous)
2. d (dogmatic:dogma)
3. c (dogmatic:dogmatism)
4. e (garrulous:taciturn)
5. c (cynical:sarcastic)
6. c (ostentation:unostentatious)
7. e (taciturnity:reticent)
8. d (ferocious:truculent)
9. e (fastidious:undiscriminating)
10. c (valid:validate)

## Unit Test   *(Word Wealth Testing Program)*

1. g (arrogant);   c (captious)
2. y (validity);   a (unctuous)
3. bb (ostentation);   p (cynicism)
4. m (aggressive);   j (dogmatic)
5. b (supercilious);
   w (scrupulousness)
6. o (officiousness);
   r (truculence)
7. d (sardonic);   aa (pessimism)
8. x (melodrama);
   s (contentiousness)
9. z (garrulousness);
   cc (effusiveness)
10. t (fluency);   v (volubility)
11. e (taciturn);   i (fastidious);
    h (misanthropic)
12. l (volatile);   u (infatuation)

# unit six

## A THRILLER

1. fortuitous, annihilate
2. instigate
3. auspicious
4. propitiate
5. egregious, aggravate
6. expedient
7. capitulate
8. extenuate

## VERBS

### 1. adumbrate

*Adumbral* (shadowy) is sometimes used. *Adumbrator* is the person form.

### 2. aggravate

Other –grav– words from Latin *gravis*, heavy, include *gravity, grave* (meaning serious, dark, heavy), and *gravamen* (a grievance)—but not *gravel, engrave,* or *gravy!* It is an odd coincidence that the Old-English-derived noun, *grave,* should appear to be a form of the adjective *grave* from Latin.

### 3. annihilate

The Latin root of *annihilate* is *nihil*, nothing. *Nihilism* is a philosophy denying that there is any valid basis for knowledge.

### 4. capitulate

The Latin root is *caput, capitis,* head, from which come *capital* (all variants), *capitol, capitation* (act of counting heads or a tax of a certain amount per person), and *per capita*.

### 5. extenuate

*Tenuous* (thin, unsubstantial, or even precarious) comes from the same Latin root, *tenuis*, thin. *Tenuousness* is the noun form.

### 6. fulminate

The person form, *fulminator,* is often used, and the adjective form, *fulminatory,* is available. A *fulminant* condition in a disease is one developing suddenly and acutely.

## 7. instigate

The word derives from Latin *instigare,* to goad, prick. *Sting, stick,* and *stigma* are words etymologically related and traceable to the same root in the hypothetical primitive Indo-European language.

## 8. mitigate

*Mitigate* comes from the Latin root, *mitis,* mild. *Mitigate* and *immitigable* are useful variants.

## 9. procrastinate

The Latin root, *cras,* tomorrow, has few projections in English.

## 10. propitiate

The word has the same root, *petere,* to seek, as *impetuous* (WW p. 221). *Propitiator, propitiatory,* and *propitiative* are often used, especially *propitiator.*

# ADJECTIVES

## 1. auspicious

*Auspicious* is one of the –spic– words (WW p. 342). The source of *auspicious* is Latin *auspex,* a Roman priest who sought omens in the flight of birds, and *auspex* comes from *avis,* bird, and *spicere,* to see. Variants include *auspicate* (to inaugurate or make a good beginning).

## 2. egregious

Words which mark one as remarkably good, distinguished, outstanding, or creditable include *exemplary* or even *stellar. Epochal* is used of events, but it is hard to find a positive word which is as forceful as *egregious* on the negative side of individualism.

## 3. equivocal

The word derives from Latin *aequus,* equal, plus *vocare,* to call. An *equivocator* is a person who is deliberately vague, ambiguous, or inclined to quibble or cavil.

## 4. expedient

*Expedient* is one of a word family built on –ped–, foot. The force of the root is more apparent in *expedite, expediter, expedition, expeditionary,* and *expeditious,* but with ironic effect in a group of words each of which to a greater or lesser degree indicates speed. *Expedite* means literally to free one caught by the feet.

5. **fortuitous**

   The basic element is –fort–, from Latin *fors, fortis,* luck or chance. *Fortuity* is an alternative noun form. *Fortuitism* is a philosophical term for the idea that natural occurrences are the result of chance rather than of design.

6. **intrinsic**

   The word, which came into English from the French, derives from Latin *intrinsecus,* inward, on the inside. The adverb form, *intrinsically,* is often used, but the alternative adjective variant, *intrinsical,* is a word one sees only in a dictionary.

7. **mystical**

   The word comes through Latin from Greek *mystikos,* belonging to secret rites, from *mystes,* one initiated. *Mystical* may mean spiritually meaningful or enigmatic, as in the expression "the mystical Communion bread of a church." It has a wide-spread nonreligious use as an approximate synonym of *psychic.* *Mystique* has a lighter sense, meaning the certain inexplicable fascination a person or institution may possess, and *mystify* means to puzzle or bewilder someone, often intentionally.

8. **sacrilegious**

   *Profanation* and *desecration* are synonyms of *sacrilege,* the former denoting chiefly thoughts or actions expressing contempt for something sacred, the latter being usually an outward act against a sacred spot or object.

9. **salubrious**

   Both *salubrious* and *salutary* come from the Latin word *salus,* health.

10. **synthetic**

    The word comes from Greek *synthetikos,* from *syn–,* with, together, plus *tithenai,* to place. The verb form *synthesize* should be mentioned: "Scientists at about the time of World War II learned to synthesize both gasoline and rubber."

# KEYS

## First Practice Set

1. propitiate, extenuate
2. fulminate, mystical
3. expedient, capitulate
4. salubrious, mitigating
5. synthetic, intrinsic
6. equivocal, sacrilegious
7. fortuitous, auspicious
8. egregious, annihilate
9. instigated, adumbrated
10. procrastinate, aggravate

## Second Practice Set

1. tenuous, augment
2. extirpate, allay
3. atone, salutary
4. cryptic, propitious
5. extrinsic, placate/mollify
6. attenuate, alleviate
7. mollify/placate, enigmatic
8. assuage, obliterate
9. exterminate, eradication
10. nihilist, rational

## Third Practice Set

1. c (aggravate—alleviate)
2. a (fortuitous—expediency)
3. d (assuaged—obliterate)
4. b (cryptic—mitigate)
5. d (eradicate—capitulation)
6. a (instigate—sacrilege)
7. c (egregious—procrastinate)
8. d (auspicious—mollify)
9. b (equivocate—assuage)
10. b (extenuate—expiate)

## A Word for It

1. eradicate, procrastinate
2. synthesis, atone
3. expedient, fortuitous
4. intrinsic, propitious
5. mitigate, egregious

## Unit Test (Word Wealth Testing Program)

1. y (procrastinate); u (aggravate); m (mitigation)
2. w (adumbrate); s (propitiate)
3. n (fulminations); c (auspicious)
4. z (augment); cc (exacerbate)
5. aa (allay); bb (obliterate)
6. l (instigation); q (nihilist)
7. r (extirpation); g (fortuitous)
8. a (intrinsic); j (mystical)
9. i (expedient); b (equivocal)
10. f (synthetic); x (alleviate)
11. k (salubrious); d (extrinsic)
12. h (enigmatic); t (extenuate)

# unit seven

## WHICH WORD?

1. curator
2. bourgeois
3. virtuoso
4. connoisseur
5. mentor
6. nemesis
7. mercury
8. coterie
9. debutante
10. liaison

## EIGHT WORDS OF FRENCH FAME

1. **bourgeois**

   The word literally means villager (from French *bourg*, town or village) and thus a provincial kind of person, as well as middle class and typically a shopkeeper.

2. **connoisseur**

   Like *recognizance* and the French-derived words *reconnoiter* and *reconnaissance*, this word comes from the Latin verb *cognoscere*, to know.

3. **coterie**

   The word comes from the French word *cote*, hut, and seems to be related to the Old English word *cot*, meaning cottage.

4. **critique**

   Derived from Greek *kritikos*, from *krinein*, to judge, discern, *critique* is sometimes used for the art of criticizing as well as a specific piece of criticism.

5. **debutante**

   The masculine form, *debutant*, is used of a person making a debut or a formal beginning of some kind.

6. **intrigue**

   The Latin root, *intricare*, is the root also of *intricate*. *Intrigant* and *intrigante* are agent forms for a person engaged in plotting or intrigue.

7. liaison

The word is derived from French *lier,* to bind. *Inamorata* (a sweetheart or mistress) is another word that pertains to love affairs, either licit or illicit. *Inamorato* is the masculine form.

8. repertoire

This is the French form of the Late Latin *repertorium,* inventory, from *reperire,* to find, acquire. *Repertory* may be used for a repository or for a collection.

## SIX WORDS FROM NAMES

1. malapropism

The word was well chosen, with the element *prop* suggesting the word *appropriate* and its root *proprius,* one's own, and with *mala* being a corruption of *mal(e),* bad.

2. mentor

The word Solon (a wise ruler), comes from Solon, Athenian statesman and lawgiver of the sixth century B.C., who framed a democratic set of laws still widely admired.

3. mercury

The first newspapers in England appeared during the civil wars in 1643. *Mercurius Aulicus* came out as a Royalist paper and *Mercurius Britannicus* soon rose up to counter it. Neither was much more than a news bulletin.

4. nemesis

Compare *harpy* (a grasping, ruthless person). The Harpies in Greek mythology were female monsters with wings and talons who abducted the souls of the dead and took the food of their victims. They were marauders and not avengers, however.

5. protean

Compare *Olympian,* meaning godlike, exalted; and *herculean,* requiring enormous strength or courage.

6. stentorian

*Volcano,* from Vulcan, the Greek form of the god of fire, with its connotations of noise, is an appropriate partner for *stentorian. Circean* (bewitching or irresistible) may be injected as an additional example of a word from a mythological name. It was Circe who turned Odysseus and his men into swine.

# SIX WORDS FROM FINE ARTS

1. **allegory**

    The word comes from Greek *allegoria,* description of one thing under the image of another. *Allegorize* is an important variant, and *allegorist* is a person form that often appears in discussions of allegory. The Irish satirist, Jonathan Swift, was an allegorist.

2. **ballet**

    The word comes, through French, Italian, and Latin, from the Greek word *ballezein,* to dance. *Ball* (a dance), *ballad* (a story-poem meant to be sung), *ballade* (a stanzaic pattern), and of course, *ballerina,* come from the same source. A *balletomane* is a ballet enthusiast.

3. **curator**

    The word is derived from Latin *curare,* from *cura,* care. A related word is *impressario,* the director of an opera or a ballet company, who may be organizer, manager, or both.

4. **denouement**

    The ending of a concert or a symphony is the *finale*.

5. **symmetry**

    The word from from Greek syn–, with, plus *metron,* a measure. *Ensemble* is a somewhat analogous term for the total effect. It is used especially in music for all the instruments or voices together or for a group of musicians who perform together, or for the entire company in a theater.

6. **virtuoso**

    Compare *prima donna* (the leading lady in an opera or concert).

# KEYS

**First Practice Set**

1. debutante, bourgeois
2. coterie, connoisseurs
3. mentor, liaison
4. curator, malapropism
5. denouement, ballet
6. repertoire, stentorian
7. nemesis, allegory
8. *Mercury,* critique
9. protean, virtuoso
10. intrigue, symmetry

**Second Practice Set**

1. savant, junta
2. nuncio, arbiter
3. parvenu, inapropos
4. patrician, epicure
5. cabal, coup d'etat
6. sage, clique
7. tutor, ingenue
8. gourmet, treatise
9. repertoire, plebeian
10. emissary, disquisition

## Third Practice Set

1. a (connoisseur: ballet)
2. d (Proteus: variability)
3. c (mentor: virtuoso)
4. b (choreographer: ballet)
5. c (cabal: junta)
6. d (curator: museum)
7. d (Mercury: mercurial)
8. d (aristocrat: patrician)
9. d (sage: savant)
10. b (patrician: aristocracy)

## Bonus

1. proletarian, liaison
2. debut, inapropos
3. allegorical, nemesis
4. symmetry, intrigues
5. mercurial, virtuosity

## Word Hunt

2. Some additional words from mythological names include:
   atlas—from Atlas, who literally carried the world on his shoulders
   erotic—from the Greek god Eros, god of love
   martial—from the Roman god of war, Mars
   cupidity—from Cupid, by a shift of meaning (see WW p. 249)
   herculean—from Hercules

3. Reconnaissance—an exploratory military survey of enemy territory
   Croquet—a lawn game in which players take turns driving a wooden ball with a mallet through a series of arches
   A debacle—a disaster, collapse, or downfall
   Ballet Russe—a famous company of Russian ballet artists
   Billet-doux—an older term for a love letter, literally a "sweet letter"
   Claque—a group of admirers, especially a noisy group hired to applaud at a performance
   Allegorist—a person who writes or has written an allegory
   Asymmetry—a lack of symmetry or balanced arrangement of parts
   Savoir faire—a form of "sophistication" that consists of knowing what to do in various situations, particularly social ones
   A virtuoso—a gentleman who dabbled in science and the arts
   Belles lettres—an older French term for literature, meaning "pretty or polite letters"

## Unit Test *(Word Wealth Testing Program)*

1. i (debutante); m (connoisseur)
2. y (parvenu); t (mentor)
3. e (mercurial); s (patrician) bb (clique)
4. o (curator); a (bourgeois)
5. z (nuncio); v (liaison)
6. x (denouement); aa (intrigue)
7. f (protean); c (stentorian)
8. g (allegorical); q (nemesis)
9. l (treatise); b (symmetrical)
10. h (repertoire); u (virtuoso)
11. p (cabal); k (pundit)
12. r (coterie); n (malapropism)

# unit eight

## CRUCIAL DISTINCTIONS

1. b (easy to get along with)
2. c (polite)
3. a (instinctive knowledge)
4. c (deceptive)
5. d (a standard of judgment)
6. b (diplomacy)
7. a (decisive)
8. c (exaggeration)
9. a (indifferent)
10. d (harmful to health)

## DISTINCTIVE NOUNS

1. **amenity**

   The word comes, through French, from Latin *amoenus,* pleasant. *Amenability* is a noun form sometimes used. *Tractable, docile,* and *compliant* may be cited as synonyms of *amenable.*

2. **criterion**

   The similarity to *critique* (WW p. 237) in form, root, and meaning may be pointed out. *Criterion* comes from Greek *kriterion,* means of judging.

3. **hyperbole**

   The Greek root, *hyperballein,* means to throw beyond and is the root also of *hyperbola* (the curve formed by a section of a cone that makes a greater angle with the base than the side of the cone does).

4. **integrity**

   *Probity* may be brought in as a synonym connoting honor and moral soundness that has been well demonstrated. *Veracity,* on the other hand, is simply truthfulness and does not necessarily include probity or integrity.

5. **intuition**

   Derived from Latin *intueri,* to look on, *intuition* is teaching from within—or from supernatural sources "above" or "below." *Intuit* is a verb form sometimes used; *intuitionism* (*intuitivism*) is the philosophical belief that knowledge of reality is obtainable only by intuition.

### 6. nonchalance

This is another of the words having no recognized positive form. The Latin root is *calere,* to be warm or fervent, which also appears in *calorie* and other heat words. It follows that *nonchalance* is a "cool" word.

### 7. optimism

The word derives from Latin *optimum,* the best. *Optimize* is listed in dictionaries but rarely seen elsewhere.

### 8. pertinacity

*Tenacity* is presented on p. 99 of *Word Wealth* and the word element tain, ten(t) in *Word Wealth,* p. 298.

### 9. pessimism

The word comes from Latin *pessimus,* worst, from *pejor,* worse. A *jeremiad* is a disconsolate lament, often denunciatory, and thus pessimistic in effect. The word comes, of course, from the name of the prophet Jeremiah, who foretold disaster for his people. Few, however, believed him, and he was persecuted as a traitor.

### 10. rapacity

The Latin root is *rapere,* to seize.

## PRECISE ADJECTIVES

### 1. clandestine

The root is the Latin word *clam,* secret or hidden. Yet the English word *clam* derives from an Old English and, farther back, a Greek word *klamm,* a cramp or fetter. Thus the apparent relationship between *clandestine* and *clam* is wholly fortuitous.

### 2. coherent

The –here–, –hes–, word elements are presented in *Word Wealth* on p. 280.

### 3. compatible

The Latin root pati–, to suffer, is also the root of *compassion,* derived from the past participle, *passus.* Compare *amenable,* which indicates the willingness of one person to accept a situation or requirement, with *compatibility* (the mutual acceptance or harmony of two persons, situations, or ideas).

4. **concomitant**

   The Latin roots are *comitari,* to accompany, and *comes,* companion. Thus *concomitant* factors accompany each other like two companions traveling together on the ins and outs of the same route.

5. **crucial**

   Note that *crux* is an English as well as a Latin word. *Cruciferous* (cross bearing) may be added to the list of "cross" words.

6. **deleterious**

   The Greek root, *deleter,* means a destroyer.

7. **impervious**

   Three other –vi– words, *devious, obvious,* and *trivial,* are listed in *Word Wealth* on p. 341.

8. **iridescent**

   *Excrescent* (superfluous, appearing abnormally) may be added to the –escent list. Also *tumescent* (swelling, becoming swollen) and *rubescent, erubescent* (reddish, blushing), *convalescent, recrudescent, phosphorescent* and, of course, *effervescent.*

9. **peremptory**

   The Latin root *emere,* to take or buy, is the root of *preempt* (seize or purchase before anyone else can) and of *exempt* (freed from an obligation). Recall *caveat emptor,* the pretest caption on p. 86 of *Word Wealth.*

10. **specious**

    The root *species,* appearance, links it with the words from –spic–, and –spec– (WW p. 342).

# KEYS

## First Practice Set

1. crucial, hyperbole
2. amenities, iridescent
3. criterion, integrity
4. intuition, deleterious
5. clandestine, peremptory
6. pertinacity, rapacity
7. pessimism, coherent
8. nonchalance, compatible
9. specious, impervious
10. optimism, concomitant

## Second Practice Set

1. rectitude, intractability
2. splenetic, disconsolate
3. optimum, insidious
4. phosphorescent, mephitic
5. comity, unremitting
6. diplomacy, ostensible
7. incongruous, civility
8. litotes, consonant
9. recalcitrance, surreptitious
10. kaleidoscopic, recrudescence

**Third Practice Set**

1. c (criterion—integrity)
2. a (intuition—optimism)
3. b (amenities—diplomacy)
4. d (coherent—compatible)
5. b (clandestine—crucial)
6. b (specious—deleterious)
7. c (unwavering—splenetic)
8. a (hyperbole—pessimism)
9. c (impervious—nonchalance)
10. c (pessimism—unintegrated)

## Unit Test  *(Word Wealth Testing Program)*

1. ee (integrity);  x (criterion)
2. z (amenity);  bb (hyperbole)
3. o (nonchalant);  e (impervious)
4. i (coherent);  r (surreptitious)
5. l (compatible);  q (incongruous)
6. dd (optimism);  n (splenetic)
7. w (pertinacity);  v (rectitude)
8. a (concurrent);  p (concomitant)
9. k (specious);  cc (buoyancy)
10. h (peremptory);  u (intractability)
11. j (crucial)
12. s (rapacity);  g (deleterious)
13. c (saturnine);  f (melancholy)

## unit nine

### APPLICATIONS

1. obsolete  2. indigenous  3. hibernate  4. indigent  5. ribald
6. amortize  7. onerous  8. amalgamate  9. mundane  10. connive

### EXECUTIVE OPTIONS

1. **abrogate**

   *Abrogate* is one of the –rog– words, from *rogare*, to ask, presented in *Word Wealth* on p. 306.

2. **adulterate**

   *Ersatz* is a related German word which came into English during World War II. It means an inferior substitute for the material or item ordinarily used.

3. **alleviate**

   The Latin root *levis*, light, gives us *levity* (WW p. 170), *levigate* (to make a smooth paste of) and *levitate* (to cause to rise in the air).

4. **amalgamate**

   *Amalgamate* comes from a Greek word, *malagma*, a softening substance. The person form *amalgamator* is often used, and there are two adjective forms, *amalgamative* and *amalgamable*.

5. **amortize**

   *Amortization* and the adjective form, *amortizable,* may be mentioned. Amortization tables are obtainable from a bank or a realtor.

6. **connive**

   *Conniver* is the agent form.

7. **effect**

   This word is frequently confused with *affect,* which means to influence, to produce an effect on. *Effect* comes from Latin *efficere*, to bring about, from ex– plus *facere*, to make, do.

## 8. hibernate

The word comes from Latin *hibernare*, to pass the winter. A *hibernaculum* is a natural covering to protect a plant during the winter, such as a bud or bulb, or a shelter inhabited by a dormant animal.

## 9. pacify

Other forms from Latin *pax*, peace, include *pacifiable, pacified, pacifistic, pacificator*, and *pacificatory*.

## 10. stultify

The word is derived from Latin *stultus*, foolish. In law to *stultify* a person means to assert that the person is of unsound mind and therefore not legally responsible.

# QUALITIES AND CONDITIONS

## 1. clement

*Clement* and *Clementine* are name forms of this word derived from Latin *clemens*.

## 2. indigenous

The word sometimes means *innate* or *inherent* when used of the qualities a person possesses.

## 3. indigent

The root is the Latin verb *egere*, to need, and the *d* lingers from indu–, an older form of in–.

## 4. mundane

It comes from the Latin word *mundus*, the world, which is *le monde* in French. *Demimonde* is a term for women on the fringes of respectable society.

## 5. obsolete

The Latin root is *solere*, to become accustomed, and *ob–* has a negative force. *Solere* is also the root of *insolent*.

## 6. onerous

The Latin root *onus* appears also in *exonerate* (WW p. 124).

7. **reputable**

*Reputation* (what people think a person is) should also be listed as a variant form.

8. **ribald**

The word, of Germanic origin, came into English from Old French *ribauld,* wanton, rascal, from *riber,* to be wanton. *Obscenity* is generally more offensive and less amusing than *ribaldry. Vulgarity* denotes bad taste and coarseness. *Grossness* is brutish and rude.

9. **traumatic**

The word *trauma* comes bodily from Greek and means a violent shock or wound. *Traumatism* is a longer form of the same word for the abnormal condition brought about by a trauma.

10. **voluptuous**

*Voluptuous* comes from the Latin word *voluptas,* pleasure. *Ascetic* is a too inclusive antonym, a more perfect opposite for *hedonist. Continent,* on the other hand, is too narrow an antonym for *voluptuous.*

# KEYS

## First Practice Set

1. indigent, amalgamate
2. effect, amortize
3. pacify, abrogate
4. connive, onerous
5. indigenous, traumatic
6. mundane, ribald
7. adulterate, alleviate
8. obsolete, reputable
9. voluptuous, stultify
10. clement, hibernate
11. effected, alleviate
12. onerous, pacify

## Second Practice Set

1. disreputable, hedonistic
2. pacifists, eventuality
3. impecunious, epicurean
4. ludicrousness, archaic
5. effectuation, destitute
6. coalescence
7. inclement, aestivate, execution
8. ameliorate, lenient
9. integration, conspires
10. disrepute, impoverished

## Third Practice Set

1. c (affluent:indigent)
2. d (lenient:mitigate)
3. a (ribald:sacred)
4. c (integrate:amalgamate)
5. b (alleviation:assuagement)
6. d (eternal:temporal)
7. a (consummate:stultify)
8. c (sectarian:secular)
9. d (indigent:destitute)
10. c (abrogate:consummate)

## A Word for It

1. onerous, impoverished/indigent
2. traumatic, pacifist
3. collusion, ribaldry
4. destitute, mundane
5. nonsectarian, secular

## Unit Test  *(Word Wealth Testing Program)*

1. w (connive);  ee (pacify)
2. bb (abrogate);  dd (alleviate);  y (adulterate)
3. p (collusion);  aa (effect)
4. a (indigenous);  f (aboriginal)
5. k (impecunious);  c (destitute)
6. i (secular);  e (decadent)
7. v (hibernate);  z (aestivate)
8. u (interfusion);  o (coalescence)
9. b (indigent);  h (impoverished)
10. j (clement);  l (unalloyed)
11. t (consolidation);  n (amortization)
12. s (stultification);  q (eventuality)

# unit ten

## CREDO FOR HARD WORK

1. tantamount  2. analogy  3. pragmatic  4. peripheral  5. anomaly
6. allergic  7. accolade  8. adamant  9. exigency  10. catholic

## NOUNS FOR SPECIAL USES

1. **accolade**

    Through the French word *accoler*, to embrace, the word can be traced back to Latin *accollare*, from ad– plus *collum*, neck. One form of *accolade* is *kudos*, a colloquial term for honorary degrees conferred by colleges and universities each year on distinguished persons in various fields of science, industry, and letters.

2. **amnesty**

    The word may also be used as a verb.

3. **analogy**

    The word is derived from Greek ana– plus *logos*, reason, ratio, from *legein*, to gather, speak. A verb form, *analogize*, and a person form, *analogist*, are often used. One might point out that analogies can be used to illustrate anything but are valueless as proofs.

4. **anomaly**

    *Anomalistic* is an adjective form, applicable to a manner or method of thinking or acting. The root is the Greek word *homos*, the same, preceded by the negative prefix an– (see homo– words WW p. 352).

5. **exigency**

    The Latin root is *agere*, to act, do, or drive. It is the root of *act*, *agent*, and numerous other words in English.

6. **franchise**

    *Franchise* comes from an Old French word *franc*, free, but before that from the Latin *francus*, free, and that in turn from *Francus*, a Frank and thus a free man because the Franks were the ruling class in Gaul in Caesar's day. Compare the name *Frank*, the adjective *frank*, and the *franking* of letters.

7. **hegemony**

   The word comes almost bodily from Greek. It has a rarely seen adjective form *hegemonic*.

8. **iconoclasm**

   *Iconography* is the study of pictorial representation or the study of a specific collection of pictures and images. *Iconolatry* is the worship of images.

9. **nepotism**

   The word comes from the Latin word *nepos*, nephew.

10. **therapy**

    The Greek root of *therapy* is *therepeia* and *therapeuein*, to care for or cure.

# ADJECTIVE ASPECTS

1. **adamant**

   The root is the Greek verb *damen*, to subdue, with the negative a– as a prefix.

2. **allergic**

   The word is derived from Greek *allergie*, from *allos*, other, plus *ergon*, work. An *allergist* is an expert in treating allergies. An *allergenic* substance is one capable of producing allergies.

3. **catholic**

   *Catholic* is one of the *holo–* (whole) words from the Greek adjective *holos*.

4. **halcyon**

   This is a poetic word with a pretty history but no variant forms.

5. **histrionic**

   The word comes from the Latin *histrio*, actor.

6. **peripheral**

   The word comes, through Old French and Late Latin from Greek *periphereia*, to carry around (the outer edge), from peri–, around and *pherein*, to carry. *Perimetric* may be substituted for *peripheral* in most cases, but the former is used in a more technical geometric sense.

7. **pragmatic**

   The root is the Greek word *pragma*, business or thing accomplished.

8. **tantamount**

   The word comes from the Latin *tantus*, so much, and the Old French word *amonter*, amount. The sense is thus "as much in amount." Other tanta– words include *tantalize* (from Tantalus, who was tormented by water he could never drink and fruit he could never reach) and *tantalization* (WW p. 81).

9. **utopian**

   *Idyllic* is a near synonym, but it is a poetic word and utopias are as a rule decently pragmatic in concept. *Elysian* and *ambrosial* are also poetic and qualitative rather than utopian in significance.

10. **vicarious**

    The root is the Latin *vicis*, a change or alteration. The noun form *vicariousness* is commonly used.

# KEYS

**First Practice Set**

1. accolade, iconoclasm
2. amnesty, therapy
3. franchise, utopian
4. exigency, histrionic
5. allergic, vicariously
6. catholic, analogy
7. peripheral, halcyon
8. tantamount, nepotism
9. adamant, pragmatic
10. hegemony, anomaly

**Second Practice Set**

1. amnesia, erratic
2. empirical, rational
3. El Dorado, New Atlantis
4. vicar, protagonist
5. antagonist, allegory
6. tangential, Republic
7. therapeutics, hydrotherapy
8. eulogy, superficial
9. disenfranchisement, iconology
10. capricious, parable

**Third Practice Set**

1. a (Thespian:histrionic)
2. c (adamant:diamond)
3. a (pragmatic:empirical)
4. d (analogy:allegory)
5. c (therapy:psychotherapy)
6. c (iconoclast:iconoclasm)
7. d (peripheral:tangential)
8. b (exigency:pragmatist)
9. b (erratic:capricious)
10. b (New Atlantis:Utopia)

**A Word for It**

1. catholicity, iconoclasm
2. pragmatic, analogy
3. therapeutic, vicariously
4. allergy, exigency
5. histrionic, sanative

## Logophile Licks

1. Ana–, a prefix derived through Latin from Greek, has a variety of meanings: up, upward, as in *anadromous* and *analects;* throughout, thoroughly, as in *analysis;* back, backwards, as in *anagram;* again, as in Anabaptist (one baptized again); according to, similar to, as in *analogy;* and against, as in *anachronism.* Other ana– words include *anabiosis* (resuscitation); *anabolism* (process of changing food into living tissue); *anaclitic* (leaning, dependent upon); *anapestic, anastrophe* (inversion or reversal of normal word order in a sentence); *anathema; anatomy, anatomize* (cut up).

2. Idio–, from Greek *idios*, own, private, is a combining form meaning one's own; peculiar to a person or thing; individual. The effect of the prefix on such words as *idiocy, idiom, idiomatic, idiomorphic, idiosyncrasy,* and idiot is readily seen.

3. Terms pertaining to Greek drama:

    skena—the long low structure toward the rear of the stage that served as background.
    proscenium—the stage of an ancient theater; the part of a modern theater in front of the curtain.
    strophe—the movement of the chorus in a Greek theater in turning from the right to the left side of the stage, thus the lines spoken during this interval and, today, a section or stanza of a poem, especially one containing sections of irregular length.
    antistrophe—the counter movement from left to right or the song that accompanied it.
    peripeteia—the reversal or change of fortune that takes place for the protagonist, usually dramatic and sudden. Ideally it coincides with the recognition scene.
    choregus—the man who sponsored and to some degree managed the production of a Greek play. He was usually the leader of the chorus.
    deus ex machina—a "god from the machine," by which a Greek playwright sometimes solved the protagonist's otherwise insoluable problems by bringing a god or goddess down on the stage.
    anagnorisis—the recognition scene in which the protagonist learns the truth.
    hamartia—the tragic fault causing the suffering and pain which the protagonist must endure.

4. Ten possible examples are:

    | | | | |
    |---|---|---|---|
    | activist | activism | Marxist | Marxism |
    | altruist | altruism | optimist | optimism |
    | anarchist | anarchism | pacifist | pacifism |
    | enthusiast | enthusiasm | pessimist | pessimism |
    | hypnotist | hypnotism | theist | theism |

Many words like *truism* have no familiar –ist form; and many –ist words like *scientist, physicist, therapist,* and *archeologist* have no –ism form or have one that is seldom used.

5. Such words as the following might be listed:

   hegemonizer—one who arranges or negotiates hegemony.
   commnesty—act of remembering collectively.
   histriotherapy—acting in plays as a cure for physical or mental ills. The term socio-drama is often used.

## Unit Test   *(Word Wealth Testing Program)*

1. w (accolade);   r (panegyric)
2. o (amnesty);
   z (disenfranchisement)
3. t (hegemony);   x (anomaly)
4. d (allergic);   p (exigency)
5. y (nepotism);
   bb (iconoclasm)
6. h (pragmatic);   k (empirical)
7. b (thespian);   m (therapeutic);
   a (vicarious)
8. j (utopian);   aa (protagonist)
9. v (iconology);
   u (resemblance)
10. n (halcyon);   c (Saturnian)
11. e (catholic);   i (adamant)
12. g (peripheral);   cc (analogy)

# part four

## unit one

### QUERIES

1. writing
2. through
3. breath
4. moving, toward
5. across
6. before
7. sticking
8. around
9. bending
10. behind

### PREFIXES OF DIRECTION

1. **ad–**

   This is the Latin preposition *ad*, with the meaning unchanged. More than 200 examples are listed under the form ad– in an average college dictionary.

2. **circum– ... peri–**

   Some fifty examples of words with circum– at the beginning may be found in a college dictionary. In addition there are negative opposites like *uncircumscribed*. Compare *circa*, about.

   Peri–, the Greek counterpart of the Latin preposition *circum*, has about fifty examples, including *period* (peri– plus *hodos*, way), plus a few prefix opposites. It may occasionally be confused with per–, through, in words like *perish*. Among the most familiar peri– words are *perigee* (point nearest earth in the orbit of a heavenly body), *perihelion* (orbit point nearest the sun), and *peripatetic* (walking around).

3. **in–**

   More than 1,500 words beginning with in– (plus hundreds more starting with il–, im–, and ir–) can be found in a college dictionary.

4. **per–**

   More than 200 examples may be found in a college dictionary plus an equal number in chemical terminology.

5. **re–**

   Re– is the initial syllable of at least 1,000 of the words listed in a college dictionary.

*155*

### 6. trans–

Occasionally shortened to tra–, trans– is the first syllable of some 200 words, and it appears in dozens of prefix antonyms like *untransformed* or *untransmitted*.

## PREFIXES OF TIME WHEN

### 1. pre– . . . ante–

More than 400 words in a college dictionary begin with pre–, and many prefix opposites like *unpremeditated* swell the total number of pre– words.

Ante– has a much more limited incidence, however, with but one or two dozen examples, some of which, like *anticipate,* are not readily distinguished from examples of anti–, against.

### 2. pro–

Its range of meanings is greater than that of most prefixes from Latin prepositions. Some 500 examples may be found, with at least an equal number of prefix opposites like *disproportionate* and *unprofitable*. In addition there are many words like *reproduce* and *reprocessing* having an additional prefix.

### 3. post–

The incidence of this prefix is limited to perhaps 200 examples.

## ACTION ROOTS FROM LATIN

### 1. –cede–, –ceed–, –cess–. . . –gredi–, –gress–

*Ingress, egress,* and their variants may be added. A comprehensive list of examples from these two roots, including all variant forms, would certainly run as high as 200.

### 2. –flect–, –flex–

*Deflect* and its variants may be added.

### 3. –fract– . . . –rupt–

*Diffract* may be added, also *corrupt, interrupt,* and *abrupt.*

### 4. –fuse(e)–

*Refuse, confuse, suffuse,* and *effusive* are additional examples.

5. –here–, –hes–

The spelling of *adherence, coherence, inherence,* and *incoherence* may well be stressed, in contrast with *inheritance.*

6. –lude–, –lus–

*Collude, collusion,* and *illusion* (WW p. 106) may be reviewed in rounding out the ramifications of these elements.

7. –mute–

*Mutable* and *immutable* should be listed with other –able forms. *Mutual* and *mutuality* contain this element, but *mute* (unable to speak) and *mutilate* do not.

8. –scribe–, –script– . . . –graph–, –gram–

Add *ascribe, conscript, scribe, transcribe,* and *rescript* (a decree or order) to the list, with their variants. *Telegraph, autograph, phonograph, cardiogram,* and *grammar* are a few of the dozens of other words from this source.

9. –spire–, –spirat– . . . –hale–

*Respire, conspire,* and variants like *respiratory* and *conspiracy* may well be mentioned. The –hale– words are relatively few in number and do *not* include *hallucination, halo* (from Greek *halos,* threshing floor) or the halo– (salt) words in chemistry.

# KEYS

## First Practice Set

1. turn
2. after
3. ahead of time, beforehand
4. forward
5. (before) in front of
6. again
7. breathe
8. go (move) forward
9. sticks to
10. bends

## Second Practice Set

1. precede
2. antedate
3. aspire
4. infuse
5. circumscribe
6. transoceanic
7. aggressive
8. prelude
9. accession
10. infraction
11. transfusion
12. allusions
13. proscribe
14. adhesive
15. transpire
16. postscript
17. interlude
18. respiration
19. permutations
20. peroxide

158/part four

**Third Practice Set**

**A.**

| | | | |
|---|---|---|---|
| 1. 4 | 6. 3 |
| 2. 1 | 7. 12 |
| 3. 8 | 8. 7 |
| 4. 6 | 9. 11 |
| 5. 10 | 10. 5 |

**B.**

| | | | |
|---|---|---|---|
| 1. 3 | 6. 1 |
| 2. 9 | 7. 10 |
| 3. 7 | 8. 4 |
| 4. 8 | 9. 2 |
| 5. 11 | 10. 12 |

**Suffixes and Such**

1. 
| −ence | −ity | −ness | −ion |
|---|---|---|---|
| adherence | flexibility | cohesiveness | diffraction |
| persistence | mutability | corruptness | inscription |
| precedence | perceptivity | descriptiveness | interfusion |
| preference | permeability | disruptiveness | procession |
| transcendence | receptivity | elusiveness | procrastination |
| transference | transferability | recessiveness | retraction |

−or
aggressor
commutator
conspirator
inventor
reflector
retractor

2. The words are *mutable; transoceanic; adhesive; (in)flexible; cohesive; aggressive; posthumous; transatlantic; perceptive.*

## Unit Test   (*Word Wealth Testing Program*)

1. b (unite:divide)
2. d (injection:ejection)
3. c (poetry:poet)
4. b (perceptive:discerning)
5. c (antediluvian:postdiluvian)
6. c (construct:structure)
7. c (collude:collusion)
8. c (postnatal:prenatal)
9. b (inherit:inheritor)
10. d (adherence:adherent)
11. c (inhale:exhale)
12. a (mirror:reflection)
13. b (procrastination:inaction)
14. a (worshipers:genuflection)
15. d (encephalograms:brain studies)
16. d (perspiration:human body)
17. b (flexible:adaptable)
18. c (periphery:interior)
19. b (eruption:volcano)
20. a (prologue:play)

# unit two

## THE RIGHT WORD

1. preclude 2. immobilize 3. devolve 4. protract 5. conjecture
6. extort 7. retract 8. impend 9. postpone 10. absolve

## PREFIXES OF SEPARATION

1. **ab–**

   *Abolish* (WW p. 2), *abrogate* (WW p. 256), and *abstain* (WW p. 131) are ab– words, but *abridge* (WW p. 86) derives from ad–, *abyss* (WW p. 29) from the Greek negative prefix a–, and *abate* (WW p. 26) from a–, an Old English prefix.

2. **de–**

   Entry words beginning with de– are *debilitate, defer, delinquent, demeanor, demur, deprave, deprecate, depreciate, derelict, derision, desiccate, despondent, deter.*

3. **dis–**

   Entry words that begin with dis– are *disburse, discern, discretion, discriminate, disparage, disperse,* and *dissipate*, also *diverge* and *divulge*, from which the *s* has disappeared. *Deluge, defy, denouement,* and other de– words from French are also traceable to the Latin dis– by way of the French equivalent, des–, in which the *s*, being silent, has been lost.

4. **ex–, e–**

   Twenty-five entry words in *Word Wealth* begin with this element.

5. **se–**

   *Secret, secretary, seduce,* and *separate* are among the most familiar examples (see *segregate*, WW p. 61).

*160/part four*

## THREE PREFIXES OF CLOSE RELATIONSHIP

1. con–... syn–

   The con– clan runs to some 2,000 in strength, if all of the words like *inconclusive* and *reconsider*, which do not begin with col–, com–, or con–, are counted. More than one third of the entry words under *c* begin with con– or one of its variants.

2. epi–... sur–

   Epi– is of Greek origin, and it serves as a prefix for perhaps a hundred English words. These include *epiglottis, epicycle, epidemic, epitome, epistle, epigram, Epiphany,* and *epileptic*.
   
   Sur– is Latin, a simplified form of super–. *Surcharge, surface, surfeit* (WW p. 203), *surmise, surplus, surrender, surtout* (outer coat), and *survey* are familiar examples, but sur– in *surreptitious* is traced to sub–, under.

3. sub–

   Examples abound of this prefix in its various forms, and the total number of words beginning with one of them is on the order of 300. Six appear as *Word Wealth* entry words: *subjugate* (WW p. 61), *subsidize* (WW p. 196), *subterfuge* (WW p. 154), *subtle* (WW p. 109), *succinct* (WW p. 205), and *succor* (WW p. 56).

## LATIN VERB ROOTS

1. –clude–, –clus–

   *Include, conclude, occlude* may be added to the list. *Clause, claustral* and *cloister* come from the same Latin verb *claudere*, to shut or close, arising from its past participle, *clausus*, rather than from its infinitive. The names *Claude* and *Claudia* come from the Latin adjective *claudus*, lame.

2. –fact–, –fect–, ... –fict–

   This is one of the most prolific of all the Latin roots. Some fifteen derivatives appear under fact– in a college dictionary, but most are formed with prefixes.

3. –ject–

   *Inject, subject, reject,* and *object* are examples that should be added, with their variants.

4. –mit–, –miss–

   *Omit* and *intermission* should be added to the list in the text. The total number of words generated from –mit– and –miss– is unusually large.

5. −move−, −mot−, −mobil−

   *Remove, commotion, mobility,* and *remote* may also be mentioned.

6. −pend−, −pense−

   *Pending, perpendicular,* and several prefix-opposite forms like *indispensable* may be added to the list.

7. −pone−, −pose−, −posit−

   *Impose, repose,* and *suppose* may be added, with their variants.

8. −solve−, −solut−

   *Dissolve* is one of the more familiar examples. *Irresolute, absolutist,* and *absolutism* are additional prefix opposites.

9. −tort−

   *Retort* may be added. From *torquere* come also *torsion* (bars), *tort* (a wrongful act for which legal action can be brought), and *torsade,* a kind of twisted cord used in drapery.

10. −tract−

    *Subcontract* and *subtract* may also be listed. A large plane has re*tract*able landing gear.

11. −volve, −volu−

    *Volute* (spiral scroll forming the capital of a column), *involutions* (complications, intricacies), and *volvulus* (intestinal obstruction from twisted or displaced intestines) round out the −volve− words. *Volution* (a revolving, a spiral, or a convolution) is sometimes used and is not to be confused with *volition* (act of will or choice).

# KEYS

**First Practice Set**

1. send . . . away
2. draw/drag/lead
3. making . . . from
4. hang
5. twist . . . away
6. turn
7. place . . . together
8. loosening . . . from
9. shut . . . away/apart
10. casting . . . out
11. drawing . . . back
12. loosened from
13. move
14. sent out/forth
15. cast down
16. after . . . deed
17. sending . . . away
18. hang . . . under
19. draws . . . together
20. hangs to

## Second Practice Set

1. motive
2. pensive
3. dissolve
4. impends
5. extortion
6–7. exclusion, distractions
8. suspension
9. missionary
10. supposition, conjecture
11. dejection
12. fiction
13. exclusion
14. dismissal
15. demotion
16. involvement
17. compendium
18. mobilize
19. assumption
20. abstraction

## Third Practice Set

1. 10
2. 6
3. 1
4. 8
5. 5
6. 3
7. 11
8. 4
9. 12
10. 7

## Suffixes and Word-Building

1. Suffixes found in the –mit– and –miss– words are:
   –ion in *mission* and *admission* makes a word that is usually a noun, sometimes an adjective.
   –ary in *missionary* and *emissary* makes an agent noun or adjective.
   –al in *committal* and *transmittal* makes a noun or adjective.
   –ance in *remittance* and *admittance* makes a word that is usually a noun. Other suffixes that may be used are: –ible, to form words like *admissible*; –ive, to form words like *permissive*; –ness to form words like *submissiveness*; –ent to form such words as *intermittent*.

2. Words ending in –ix include, besides the familiar *prefix* and *suffix, directrix, executrix, matrix*. A word ending with –ix is usually a noun and often the feminine form of an agent word.

3. Words from –pon–, –pos–, –posit– may be tabulated thus:

| Component | compose | composition |
| exponent | expose | exposition |
| * * * | suppose | supposition |
| proponent | propose | proposition |

The two that take an –ory ending are *expository* and *suppository*. The –ory ending is an adjective ending, but the word may be used as a noun. *Composure* and *exposure* have the –ure *suffix*.

## Unit Test   *(Word Wealth Testing Program)*

1. d (imagination: actuality)
2. b (book: appendix)
3. d (attract: distract)
4. b (postpone: delay)
5. a (missionary: emissary)
6. d (conjecture: theory)
7. b (short story: fiction)
8. a (governor: pardon)
9. a (epidermis: skin)
10. d (component: television set)
11. a (strike: mediation)
12. d (conjecture: fact)
13. b (symposium: viewpoints)
14. c (exclude: include)
15. a (conjecture: surmise)
16. c (Martin Luther: Reformation)
17. d (approve: reprove)
18. c (structure: edifice)
19. a (expenditures: outlays)
20. a (affectation: folly)

# unit three

## MEANING HUNT

1. not
2. wrongly/incorrectly
3. against
4. against
5. against/contrary to
6. carry
7. drive/push . . . back/away
8. hold
9. come . . . between
10. calling together

## EIGHT NEGATIVE PREFIXES

1. **a–**

   Other examples include *achromatic* (lens), having no color fringe or aberration; *anarchy; anomaly* (WW p. 68).

2. **anti–, ant–**

   *Antiaircraft, antibacterial, antibiotic, anticlimax, antilogy* (a contradiction in ideas), and *antipodes* are additional examples. Ant(a)– words come from Greek.

3. **counter– . . . contra–**

   Counter– comes from the Latin contra– by way of French. *Counteraction, countermand* (cancel or revoke), *counterclaim, counterirritant, counterintelligence,* and *counterrevolution* are a few examples of counter– that might be added. *Contradistinction, contralto,* and *contravention* may be cited as additional examples of contra–.

4. **in–**

   *Impervious, imprecation, inane, incorrigible, inert, inexorable, inscrutable, insolence, invective* are supplementary examples.

5. **mis–**

   This prefix, from Old English, has at least one hundred examples listed in a college dictionary. Compare *misadventure, misbegotten, misconception, misdemeanor, misnomer, mistranslate.* The mis– in *misanthrope*, however, comes from a Greek root meaning hate.

6. **non–**

   The dictionary lists nearly 1,000 words beginning with non–, the Latin word for *not*. Two are entry words: *nonentity* (WW p. 98) and *nonchalance* (WW p. 248).

7. **ob–**

   *Ob* is a Latin preposition. A majority of the *Word Wealth* entry words under O are ob– words.

8. **un–**

   Un– words are even more numerous than non– words, for un– is the most widely employed of all English prefixes.

## TEN LATIN ACTION ROOTS

1. **–duce–, –ducat–, –duct–**

   This root forms a word family with each of ten different prefixes and has thus proved to be one of the most prolific of word elements in English.

2. **–fer–, –late–**

   It rivals the –duce– words in its proliferations, with more families but averaging fewer members in each one. *Elate* and *elation* are also products of –late–.

3. **–pel–, –pulse–**

   *Appellation* (name or designation) may be added to the list, as well as *appeal*, *appellate*, and their variant forms.

4. **–port–, –portat–**

   *Comport* (conduct) is an additional verb from this root that may be mentioned. *Portable, exportable*, and *insupportable* are a few of the –able words in this large family

5. **–serve–**

   *Observe* (used under ob–), *preserve, deserve,* and their variants round out the list.

6. **–sist–**

   *Transistor*, a device which stands across a radio circuit to detect, rectify, or amplify the signals that come in, should be mentioned.

## 7. –tain–, –ten(t)–

*Pertain, contain, maintain* (literally, to hold in the hand), and *sustain* serve to round out the list. *Intend* and *intentior*, however, come from the Latin verb *tendere*, to stretch out or aim for.

## 8. –vene–, –vent–

*Contravene, supervene, adventure,* and *adventitious* are additional examples. –Vent– (come) should not be confused with –vent– (wind) in *ventilate* and other "wind" words.

## 9. –vert–, –verse– . . . –verge–

*Convert, converse, pervert, perverse, subvert, subversive, obverse, animadvert, introvert, extrovert, ambivert,* and *version* are additional words from these roots. Review *diverge* (WW p. 36).

## 10. –voke–, –vocat–

*Vocal, vox populi* (voice of the people), and *equivocate* are related words from the Latin word *vox*, voice.

# KEYS

| **First Practice Set** | **Second Practice Set** | **Antonyms** |
|---|---|---|
| 1. against | 1. counter | 1. unmanageable |
| 2. not | 2. non | 2. illogical |
| 3. against | 3. anti | 3. antiseptic |
| 4. against | 4. anti | 4. unpreventable |
| 5. wrong/incorrect | 5. il | 5. misbehavior |
| 6. not | 6. mis | 6. nonconductor |
| 7. bent/shaped | 7. expel | 7. unobtainable |
| 8. call . . . forth | 8. diverg | 8. nonexistence |
| 9. keeping . . . from | 9. convocation | 9. counterproposal |
| 10. keep | 10. induce | 10. irreligious |
| 11. drive | 11. desist | |
| 12. turn | 12. deporta | |
| 13. turn | 13. ferous | |
| 14. coming | 14. inversion | |
| 15. not hold | 15. educat | |
| 16. stand | 16. retention | |
| 17. bears | 17. persist | |
| 18. carry | 18. irrevoc | |
| 19. drives | 19. incontrovert | |
| 20. lead | 20. impuls | |

**Suffixing**

1. Additional examples of prefixes:

| a– | anti–, ant– | counter–, contra– | in– |
|---|---|---|---|
| agnostic | antibiotic | contrast | illicit |
| agraphia | anticlimax | contravene | impertinent |
| anarchy | antidote | counterintelligence | innocuous |
| anoxia | antifreeze | counterrevolutionary | inimical |
| atheism | antilogy | counterpoise | irrelevant |

| mis– | non– | ob– | un– |
|---|---|---|---|
| misjudge | nonchalant | obviate | uncommunicative |
| misnomer | nonentity | occlude | unconscious |
| misspeak | nonessential | offer | unexceptionable |
| misstatement | nonmetal | oppress | ungrammatical |
| mistrust | nonrestrictive | opprobrium | unmanned |

The number of words beginning with non– in a college-size dictionary is approximately 800. About 1,700 begin with un–.

2. Some examples are:
ductile—unductile; conducive—unconducive; seductive—unseductive; soporiferous—unsoporiferous; subservient—unsubservient; retentive—unretentive; tenable—untenable; adventitious—unadventitious.

3.
| | | | |
|---|---|---|---|
| reduce | reduction | reducible | irreducible |
| deduce | deduction | deducible | undeductible |
| abduct | abduction | * * * | * * * |
| educate | education | educable | uneducable |
| conduct | conduction | conductive | unconductive |
| induct | induction | inductive | uninductive |
| induce | (inducement) | * * * | * * * |

4. Some examples are:
*coniferous*—cone-bearing; *luciferous*—providing light, figuratively or literally; *luminiferous*—giving off light; *pestiferous*—mischievous; *proliferous*—having leafy shoots; *seminiferous*—seed bearing.

5.

| –vert–, –verse– | | –port(at)– | –pel–, –pulse– |
|---|---|---|---|
| advertisement | diversion | comportment | compulsive |
| averter | inadvertent(ly) | exporter | compulsory |
| avertible | inverse(ly) | importance | expulsion |
| convergence | perverse(ly) | importunate | impulsive(ly) |
| converse | perversion | portability | propellant |
| conversion | reversal | portentous | repulsive(ly) |
| convertible | reverse | reporter | |
| divergence | revert | supporter | |

6.

| | | |
|---|---|---|
| assist | assistant | assistance |
| consist | (in)consistent | (in)consistency |
| exist | (non)existent | (non)existence |
| insist | (un)insistent | insistence |
| persist | (un)persistent | persistence |
| resist | (un)resistent | (non)resistance |

## Unit Test   *(Word Wealth Testing Program)*

1. c  (mortality:immortality)
2. c  (invoke:revoke)
3. a  (tenet:belief)
4. a  (pacifism:Quaker)
5. c  (news:noteworthy events)
6. c  (detention:police)
7. a  (expulsion:propulsion)
8. b  (repulsion:criminals)
9. a  (opium:soporiferousness)
10. d  (city:tenements)
11. a  (reduce:decrease)
12. b  (exportation:importation)
13. b  (caretaker:keys)
14. c  (destruction:construction)
15. a  (invent:devise)
16. b  (tenacity:persistence)
17. b  (science:inventors)
18. d  (counterplot:criminals)
19. b  (inconsistent:consistency)
20. c  (hobby:avocation)

# unit four

## WORD PRESCRIPTIONS

1. astringent
2. insomnia
3. colloquy
4. obstruction
5. placebo
6. mandate
7. avocation
8. parliament
9. Dictaphone
10. conjunction

## MOSTLY FOOTWORK

1. **–ambul–, –ambulat–**

   *Ambulance, ambulant,* and *ambulate* are additional words from this root.

2. **–cur(r)– . . . –curs–, –course**

   *Cursive* (writing), *discursive* (talk), *recourse,* and their variants round out the range of derivatives.

3. **–migr(a)–**

   *Remigrate* is sometimes used. *Migrator* is typical of the agent nouns that spring from the various word roots.

4. **–scend–, –scent–**

   *Descend* and *reascend* should be included. Variant forms of *ascend* include *ascendable* (or *ascendible*), *ascendant* (or *ascendent*), *ascendancy* (or *ascendency*), *ascender, ascending,* and *ascensive.* Few word families offer so wide a choice in spellings.

## MAINLY MOUTHWORK

1. **–dict–, –dictat– . . . –loqu–, –locu–**

   *Condition* comes from *dicere; eloquent* and *grandiloquent* are additional examples of –loqu–.

2. **–logue–, . . . –logy–**

   *Epilogue* and *monologue* may be added, as well as an almost endless number of –ologies. Some teachers will want to point out that *Logos,* Word, is applied to Christ in the Gospel of John (1:1) and elsewhere.

3. **–mand–**

From the Latin root, *mandare,* to command, come also *commandant* and the legal term *mandamus* (a written court order), but not *reprimand,* which comes from the Latin verb *primere,* to press.

4. **–nounce–, –nunci– . . . . –sert–**

The root of –<u>nounce</u>–, –<u>nunci</u>– is *nuntiare,* to declare or state. *Denunciator* is the agent form of *denounce, announcer* that of *announce,* and *renouncer* that of *renounce.*

5. **–parl–**

These words come from the French verb *parler,* to speak. *Unparliamentary* is available if needed, but this element has for some reason formed few compounds with prefixes.

6. **–rog– . . . –quir–, –quisit–**

The Latin verb *rogare,* to ask, is also the root of *rogue,* which meant beggar and thus asker in the sixteenth century. The words *prorogue* and *prorogation* have historical interest as the means by which the English monarch would terminate or postpone a parliament. *Inquest* might be added to the –<u>quir</u>– list.

## COOPERATIVE ACTS

1. **–don(a)–, –ded–**

The Latin root is *donus,* gift, and *dare,* to give. *Donative, donatory,* and *donator* are other derivatives.

2. **–junc(t)– . . . . –juga**

*Disjunctive* and *subjunctive* are chiefly grammatical terms. The former pertains to clauses that present a contrast or alternative and that use such disjunctive conjunctives as *but, however,* and *either . . . or.* The word *juncture* is applicable mostly to abstract situations, *junction* to material ones.

3. **–merge–, –mers–**

*Emerge* and *immerse* are antithetical, but one is used abstractly or figuratively, as a rule, the other literally. A *merganser* is a kind of fish-eating duck, so called because it dives.

4. **–plac–, . . . –placa–**

Two similar verbs with slightly different meanings are involved. One, the root of *placate,* is *placare,* to appease; the other is *placere,* to please. *Placard* comes from neither, but has been traced to the word *plaque* and thence to the Dutch word *placke,* a plate, disk, or coin.

5. −sequ−, −secut−

*Prosecute*, with its variants, is an important projection.

6. −somn− . . . −dorm−

*Somniferous, somniloquy* (sleep talking) and *somniloquist* (one who talks while asleep) are extra examples of −loqu−.

7. −stringe−, −strict−

*Constrain(t)* also comes from the Latin word *stringere*, to draw tight, and *district* comes from *distringere*. *Constringe, constringency,* and *constringent* are seldom-used derivatives from the same source.

8. −struct−

*Construct* and its family, along with *restructure*, should also be included. The Latin root is *struere*, to build. *Construe* (WW p. 181) comes from the same source.

9. −sume−, −sump(t)−

The root is the Latin verb *sumere*, to take. *Unassuming* is a negative form from this root.

10. −tend−, −tense−

*Intend, pretend, attend,* and *contend* are all examples. The Latin root is *tendere*, to stretch.

11. −vince−, −vict−

*Convict* is another important example in modern English of the Latin root *vincere*. *Victoria* (victory) belongs to the progeny of *vincere*, but *victim* (basically a person or animal killed as a sacrifice to a god) does not.

# KEYS

**First Practice Set**

1. giver
2. stretches
3. follow
4. statement
5. joins
6. sleep
7. follow
8. walk
9. appease
10. speaking
11. drawing
12. travel
13. taking
14. runnings/ invasions
15. order
16. running
17. conquer
18. declare
19. climbs
20. plunging/ joining

**Second Practice Set**

1. migrate, transcend
2. mandatory, stringent
3. immerse, dormitory
4. placate, victor
5. interrogation, resumption
6. donation, disquisition
7. courier, contradict
8. diction, extension
9. cursory, construction
10. dedication, Annunciation

**Third Practice Set**

1. 5
2. 8
3. 1
4. 7
5. 4
6. 10
7. 3
8. 12
9. 11
10. 6

**Words and Their Parts**

1. –e (Dictaphone)—usually marks a noun; actually –e is a suffix in –logue and its derivatives
   –or (dictator)—usually creates a person or agent noun
   –ial (dictatorial)—usually indicates an adjective
   –ment (indictment)—almost invariably a noun ending for a state or condition
   –(a)tion (condemnation)—almost invariably a noun ending
   –(a)cious (loquacious)—adjective ending
   –y (colloquy)—noun ending; actually a suffix in –logy and its derivatives
   –ent (grandiloquent)—adjective ending
   –ate (mandate)—forms a noun, adjective, or verb
   –(at)ory (mandatory)—makes an adjective in this case out of an –ate noun
   –ance (parlance)—a noun ending
   –ey (parley)—actually a variant of a y ending
   –(a)tive (prerogative)—an adjective ending, which often marks a noun

2. The root −stringe−, while close in literal meaning to that of −tract−, almost always carries the idea of reducing, tightening, or limiting, with the image of cords drawn tighter. The root −tract−, on the other hand, implies power to pull, drag, or draw out something.

3.  | | | | |
    |---|---|---|---|
    | construct | constructive | construction | unconstructive |
    | destruct | destructive | destruction | * * * |
    | instruct | instructive | instruction | uninstructive |
    | obstruct | obstructive | obstruction | unobstructive |

   The suffix −ly may be attached to each word in the second column. The −ible word with prefix in− is *indestructible*.

4. The following are among the most familiar:

   | | |
   |---|---|
   | ascendable | indictable |
   | convincible | invincible |
   | destructible | predictable |
   | extendible | pronounceable |
   | implacable | renounceable |

   The root which keeps its final *e* is −nounce−. The *e* is retained to indicate that the *c* is soft, not hard as in *implacable*.

5. An *interlocutory* divorce is one decreed or approved tentatively during a suit pending an official decision but not final until the papers are signed and witnessed.

## Unit Test   *(Word Wealth Testing Program)*

1. d (drowsiness:somnolence)
2. b (immigration:emigration)
3. c (parliament:legislation)
4. d (submerge:reemerge)
5. a (edifice:magnificence)
6. a (biology:university)
7. d (placid:demanding)
8. c (mandatory:obligatory)
9. b (assertion:confirmation)
10. b (logical:illogical)
11. c (migrate:nonmigratory)
12. c (emergent:coming forth)
13. b (approval:condonation)
14. a (consecration:dedication)
15. c (Shakespeare:playwright)
16. d (ascent:descent)
17. b (detachment:abrogation)
18. d (dieter:renunciation)
19. a (ascension:burial)
20. b (instruction:education)

# unit five

## FOUR-SYLLABLE WORDS

1. maternity
2. congenital
3. patrimony
4. gratuitous
5. equivalent
6. gregarious
7. jurisprudence
8. domination
9. dexterity
10. sororicide

## FAMILY AND HOME

1. −dexter−

   *Dexter* and *dextral* are adjective forms, the one used in heraldry for the right side of a shield, the other for right-handed or the right-hand side. The opposite word is *sinistral*. The word *dextrorotatory* (or *dextrorotary*) means turning or circling to the right. Except when one is talking about polarized light, the word *clockwise* is preferred because it is shorter.

2. −dom−, −domin−, −domit−

   *Predominant* is an important adjective example. The list of −dom− words may be expanded considerably.

3. −frater(n)−, −fratri−

   *Confraternity* is a word for a group of professional men or a brotherhood of some kind.

4. −mater(n)−, −matri− . . . −metro−

   *Matriarch* (a woman who rules her family or tribe) and *matriarchy* may be added. *Mater Dolorosa*, Latin for sorrowful mother, refers to Mary, the mother of Christ, at the time of His crucifixion.

5. −nasc− . . . −gen−

   Compare *renaissance,* a synonym of *renascence,* which comes by way of French and is used chiefly of a rebirth in the arts, whereas *renascence* is more often applied to a rebirth in nature. Discuss the Renaissance in Europe that began in Italy in the 14th century, spread to other countries, and lasted well into the 17th century.

6. —(o)nym— . . . —nomin—, —nomen—

*Cognomen* is a word for a co-name, *i.e.*, a surname or a family name. The word derives from Latin <u>co</u>— plus *gnomen*, alteration of *nomen*, name.

7. —pater(n)—, —patri—

The *Pater Noster* (Our Father) is the Lord's Prayer, traditionally said in Latin. The term may also mean a rosary or the beads on it which call for the Lord's Prayer. (Also *paternoster*.) A *patron* saint is one regarded as the special guardian of a person, place, or institution.

## CITIZENSHIP AND SOCIETY

1. <u>arch</u>— . . . —archeo—

Other <u>arch</u>— words include *oligarch(y)* (the rule of a few persons); *monarchy* (the rule of one person); *heptarchy* (the rule of seven); *squirearchy* (a term once coined to denote the power of the country gentry in England); and *archaic* (WW p. 260).

2. —crat—, —cracy— . . . —pot—

*Aristocracy* is the rule of the nobility or privileged class, *i.e.*, the *best* people (Greek *aristos*, best). In Plato's *Republic*, it would be the wise men or philosophers. A *potentate* is a powerful ruler.

3. —equ(i)—

Other words from –<u>equi</u>– include *equity, equivocal* (WW p. 230), *equivalent*, and *equilateral*.

4. —grati— . . . —gratu—

*Ingratiate* (to make oneself pleasing) with its variant forms should be added. Also *gratitude* and *ingrate*.

5. —greg—

Review *egregious* (WW p. 230). Add *aggregate* (the whole, gathered together).

6. —juris— . . . —jure—

The root of the –<u>jure</u>– words is *juris*, right or law. *Juridical* (from *dicere*, to say) is an adjective meaning of or pertaining to jurisprudence or judicial proceedings.

## 7. –liber–

*Liberty, libertarian,* and *liberticide* derive from *liber,* free. *Deliberate* comes from *libra,* scales.

## 8. –plen–, –plent– . . . –plete

*Implement, supplement, supply,* and *complete* come, like *complement,* from *plere,* to fill.

## 9. –polit– . . . –civi–

*Police, policy,* and *polity* come from the Latin root *politia,* administration of the state, and ultimately from the Greek *polites,* citizen, from which the –polit– words come. *Civility, civilize,* and *civilian* are supplementary –civi– words.

## 10. –popul– . . . –demo–

*Endemic* (prevalent or indigenous to a specific region) and *epidemic* (prevalent among the people) are among the examples of –demo–.

## 11. –urb– . . . –poli–

*Interurban* bus service operates between cities or towns. Baghdad is a modernized *megalopolis* where Scheherazade is almost forgotten.

# KEYS

**First Practice Set**

1. brother
2. first
3. pleasing
4. sister
5. skill
6. (the) people
7. father
8. mother
9. full
10. power
11. control/rule
12. between . . . cities
13. "born"/created/grown
14. name
15. power
16. law
17. lump/group
18. talk/speech
19. free
20. swearing

## Second Practice Set

1. urban
2. indomitable
3. equidistant
4. fraternity
5. persona non grata
6. plenitude
7. genesis
8. congenital
9. renascence
10. maternal

## Third Practice Set

1. 7
2. 4
3. 10
4. 1
5. 6
6. 12
7. 2
8. 11
9. 5
10. 8

## Suffix Series

1. *Dukedom* and *sheikdom* are words having *kingdom* as a matrix and often used with humorous implications. *Martyrdom* indicates simply the realm of martyrs.

2. 
   | –ate | –ize |
   |---|---|
   | congratulate | civilize |
   | congregate | fraternize |
   | depopulate | liberalize |
   | dominate | patronize |
   | expatriate | popularize |
   | generate | urbanize |
   | liberate | |
   | nominate | |
   | populate | |
   | repatriate | |
   | segregate | |

3. The following may be added to the words already listed in the text:
   tetrarch—ruler (governor –<u>arch</u>–) of one fourth of a province in the Roman Empire
   monarchy—a country ruled by a king
   heptarchy—government by a group of seven rulers or an alliance of seven
   oligarchy—rule by a few powerful men
   archipelago—a group of islands
   architect—one who designs buildings (literally a chief worker or fabricator)
   architectonic—of or pertaining to architecture, figuratively or literally
   architecture—the art or profession of planning buildings
   archpriest—a chief priest
   archbishop—the first or chief bishop
   archiepiscopal—of or pertaining to an archbishop(ric)
   heresiarch—the founder of a heresy or heretical sect

squirearchy—government in effect by country gentlemen or large landowners

aristocrat, aristocracy—rule by the "best" citizens (Greek *aristos*), usually the wealthy, titled class

plutocrat, plutocracy—rule of the wealthy group or class

technocrat, technocracy—rule by the group or class most skillful in science and technological organization of society

ochlocrat, ochlocracy—mob rule or one who believes in it

4. The following –nomen– and –nomin– words may be added to those already listed in the text:

cognomen—the name one is known by, family name or nickname; no suffix

denomination—category; general name; unit of value; in religion, a group of people adhering to a particular creed

denominator—the lower figure, *i.e.*, the total number of parts on which a fraction is based

renominate—the –ate makes the word a verb

nominalism—the –ism makes the word a belief, system, or doctrine; in this case the belief that abstract words (names) like *truth* or *justice* are merely names and have no realities corresponding to them

nominalistic—the –istic makes the word descriptive and thus ordinarily an adjective

nominalist—the –ist makes a word indicating a person who holds the belief denoted by nominalism

nominator—the –or makes the word a person or agent noun

## Unit Test  *(Word Wealth Testing Program)*

1. b (fraternity:brotherhood)
2. a (rigorousness:lenient)
3. d (equalize:taxes)
4. b (executor:executrix)
5. a (synonym:antonym)
6. b (paternal:maternal)
7. c (anarchy:lawlessness)
8. a (deplete:replenish)
9. a (gratifying:displeasing)
10. a (congratulate:felicitate)
11. c (autocrat:decree)
12. c (gregarious:sociable)
13. b (plenitude:abundance)
14. b (archangel:archdevil)
15. c (veracity:perjury)
16. b (plenitude:scarcity)
17. a (replenish:deplete)
18. c (gregariousness:solitude)
19. c (populous:sparse)
20. d (matriculation:expulsion)

# unit six

## COUNTDOWN

1. two
2. hundredth
3. ninety
4. eighty
5. one
6. four
7. one hundred
8. six
9. one
10. seventh
11. ten
12. one thousand

## NUMBER PREFIXES

1. **uni–, unit– . . . mono–**

   *Unit, univalve, universe, university,* and *triune* are a few words that may be added for uni–. *Monochromatic, monocracy, monogram, monogamy, monomania, monolithic,* and *monotheism* may be listed for mono–.

2. **du– . . . bi–**

   Additional words include *duet, duplex, duodecimal, duplicity; bihourly, biennial, bilabial* (having two lips), *bilateral, bimetallic, bimonthly, binoculars*—but not *binnacle*.

3. **tri–**

   *Triangular, triarchy, triplicate, triatomic, triaxila, tricentennial, triceps, tricycle, trifurcate* (having three forks or branches), *trinity,* and *trillion* are a few of the dozens of ramifications of tri–.

4. **quadr– . . . tetr–**

   *Quadrennium, quadricentennial, quadruped, quadroon, quadruple,* and *quadrillion* are good additional examples. Tetra–, the Greek element for four, occurs also in *tetragram* (four-letter word), *tetrahedron, tetralogy* (four plays), and *tetragonal*.

5. **quin– . . . pent–**

   The Latin word for five is *quinque*, the Greek *penta. Quinquagenarian, quinquennial, quintuple, quintan* (occurring every fifth day), and *quintillion* may be added to the list for *quinque*.

6. sex– . . . hex–

   *Sexennial, sexpartite, sextant, sextuple, sestet, sextet,* and *sexcentenary* will provide additional examples. In *sextile* (two heavenly bodies sixty degrees from each other) and *Sexagesima* (second Sunday before Lent) the meaning is sixty. Hex– words include *hexameron* (the six days of the Creation or a treatise on it), *hexadron,* and *hexapod.*

7. sept– . . . hept–

   One may add *septempartite, septilateral, septillion, septet,* and *septime* (the seventh position in fencing), but not *septic* or *septicemia,* which come from the Greek word *septikos,* putrefactive. The *Septuagint* (by seventy scholars) was a famous translation of the Old Testament into Greek. A similar group of hept– words would include *heptad* (group of seven), *heptahedron, heptameter,* and *heptagenarian.*

8. oct(o)– . . . octa–

   One may add *octad, octane, octahedron, octangular, octennial, octavo* (eight sheets or leaves per signature), *octet, octapod,* and *octogenarian.*

9. nona– . . . nov– . . . ennea–

   *Nonillion* is an additional example. A *nonahedron* is conceivable, and so is *nonameter,* but most of the nov– words mean new.

10. dec–, deci– . . . deca–

    Additional examples which may be cited are *decile* (statistical values based on division of a group into ten parts), *decillion, decennial, decemvirate* (power group of ten), *decagon, decahedron, decaliter* (ten liters, but a *deciliter* is one tenth of a liter).

11. cent– . . . hect–

    Cent– has many uses, but hect– appears in only a few words. Mention *sesquicentennial* (occurring every 150 years).

12. mill–, milli– . . . kilo–

    *Milliary* (roman mile of 1,000 paces), *millibar* (unit for measuring atmospheric pressure), and *millivolt* (one thousandth of a volt), may be added to the Roman list. *Kilocalorie* (1,000 calories) and *kilocycle* (1,000 cycles per second) may be added to the Greek list.

13. multi– . . . poly–

    At least one hundred multi– words may be found in a college dictionary and about eighty poly– words. Others may readily by coined if needed.

14. semi– ... demi– ... hemi–

A *demisemiquaver* is a thirty-second note; a *hemidemisemiquaver* is a sixty-fourth note. A *demiurge* is an autonomous creative spirit, often thought of as a subordinate deity.

## NUMBER-LINKED ROOTS

1. –annu–, enni–

*Annuity* (a yearly payment or an investment yielding a fixed amount) is a good supplementary example.

2. –gamy– ... –nub–, –nupt–

*Monogamy* may be mentioned. *Nubile*, said of a woman ready for marriage, comes from *nubere*, to marry (*i.e.*, veil oneself), and is one of the few examples of –nub–, a word element that more often represents *nubes*, a cloud.

3. –later–

*Quadrilateral* is often used in geometry.

4. –meter–

*Diameter*, *speedometer* (or *tachometer*), and possibly *tetrameter* will be among the first extra words mentioned. *Demeter*, the Earth Mother, comes from the Greek root of *metropolis*, *meter*, meaning mother.

5. –ped–, –pede– ... –pod–

*Pedestrian* and *cephalopod* mark the extremes among the examples that might be cited. The latter is the term for a kind of octopus and other mollusks having tentacles ("feet") that are part of the creature's head.

## KEYS

**First Practice Set**

1. seven
2. eight
3. tenth
4. five
5. two
6. three
7. six
8. four
9. one
10. eight
11. three
12. ten
13. one thousandth
14. 1,000
15. tripod
16. measures
17. nine
18. many
19. half
20. feet

## Second Practice Set

1. six
2. five
3. seven
4. five
5. four
6. seven
7. two
8. fourth
9. eight
10. ten
11. one hundred
12. one hundred
13. two
14. many sides
15. foot
16. fifty
17. three
18. many sides
19. marriage
20. one

## Third Practice Set

1. centenarian
2. perimeter
3. nonagon
4. demigod
5. pentameter
6. decalogue
7. hectometer
8. millenniums
9. polygamy
10–11. perennial, annual
12. triennial
13. bilingual
14–15. semicircle, hemisphere
16–17. polygon, polyhedron
18. November
19. podiatrist
20. kilogram

## What Is It?

1. Quadrangle—a geometric figure having four sides (literally four angles)
2. Ennead—a group of nine, especially gods in Greek mythology
3. Hexameter—verse having six metrical feet or "measures"
4. Centimeter—one hundredth of a meter
5. Polytheism—the worship of many gods
6. The Trinity—in Christian theology the Father, Son, and Holy Spirit. A trinity is any group of three closely related persons or things.
7. Duplex house—a house that accommodates two families independently
8. Unique—unusual, uncommon, or rarely seen (literally, the only one of its kind)
9. Tercentennial—the three hundredth anniversary of an event
10. Tetrahedron—a solid figure having four surfaces
11. Decathlon—an athletic contest consisting of ten events
12. Collateral—accompanying, subordinate, related, supporting (used especially of goods or property pledged or available as security for the payment of a loan)
13. Multicellular plant—one having many cells
14. Pentagon—a geometric figure having five sides
15. Nonagenarian—a person in his nineties
16. Lateral gesture—a sidewise motion or movement
17. Annual rings—the circular sections in the cross section of a tree trunk, each of which represents a year's growth
18. Multiplicity—a large number or array
19. Millipede—an insect or worm of the *Diplopoda* class having many legs but not literally a thousand
20. Demitasse—a small cup, literally half a cup

## Curiosity Pills

1. A *duodecimal* system is based on 12 instead of 10, the word being derived from the Latin word for twelve. The *duodenum* is the first part of the small intestine, *i.e.*, the part leading from the stomach to the jejunum. It was so named because its length equals the breadth of twelve fingers.

    A *binary* number system is based on a cycle of two rather than ten units. Such a system is well suited to computers because their transistorized circuits can handle two conditions or responses more reliably than ten. Their speed compensates for the long numbers of a binary system.

2. There are some 125 mono– words in a college-size dictionary, whereas there are about 80 uni– words. Pent– words number about 25 and quint– words the same, but there are hundreds of additional pent– words in chemistry.

3. 
   | **semi–** | | **hemi–** |
   |---|---|---|
   | semiannual | semifinal(s) | hemicrania |
   | semiautomatic | semimonthly | hemicycle |
   | semicircle | semiplastic | hemihydrate |
   | semicolon | semiprecious | hemiplegia |
   | semidesert | semiserious | hemistich |

4. A signature is a section of a book consisting of the pages printed on a single large sheet of paper. In folio form, the sheet is folded once, making four pages in the finished book. A quarto signature is folded twice, making eight pages. Folding the sheet a third time makes eight leaves or sixteen pages (octavo), and a fourth folding produces a signature of thirty-two pages (sixteenmo). Before binding, the signatures are gathered, and after binding, before the covers are put on, the edges are trimmed.

5. A *unigon* would have one side and would thus be a straight line.
    A *centigon* would be a geometric figure having a hundred sides.
    A *triologue* would be the same as a dialogue except that there would be three people taking part instead of two.
    *Decuplets* would be ten children from a single birth.
    The word *biquadrate* could mean every other *quadrate* or four-part division; or, on the analogy of *bimonthly,* could mean twice in each *quadrate*.
    An *octuplicate* would be one of the eight copies or transcriptions of a document.
    *Decuplet* (ten of a kind) and *biquadratic* (fourth power) and *octuplicate* may be found in *Webster's Third New International Dictionary*.
    A *hemigon* could hardly exist because half a side would be absurd in a geometric figure.
    A *sesquicentenarian* would be 150 years old.
    A *polymonocle* could not exist; the term is self-contradictory.
    *Tetralateral* is a word not needed as long as *quadrilateral* is available and well established. It is abnormal to combine a Greek prefix with a Latin root or vice versa.

## Unit Test  *(Word Wealth Testing Program)*

1. a (solo:duet)
2. c (triad:sextet)
3. d (quadrangle:octagon)
4. d (duplicate:octuplicate)
5. c (unit:decimal)
6. c (triumvirate:heptarchy)
7. d (half awake:semiconscious)
8. d (unicellular:multicellular)
9. a (soloist:orchestra)
10. b (centimeter:meter)
11. a (millimeter:meter)
12. c (bigamous:polygamous)
13. a (stampede:cattle)
14. b (yearly:year after year)
15. c (unicycle:vehicle)
16. d (Pentecost:Christian festivals)
17. a (three cornered:hat)
18. c (pentameter:poetry)
19. b (mononucleosis:disease)
20. d (heptagon:geometry)

# unit seven

## RATHER TECHNICAL

1. superlative
2. introspective
3. aquamarine
4. hyperbolic
5. interspersed
6. hypertensive
7. navigable
8. apocalyptic
9. confluent
10. petulant

## OUTWARD-INWARD PREFIXES

1. **acro–**

   The Greek root is *akros*, at the point, tip, or extremity. Thus an *acrocarpous* plant is one which bears its fruit at the end of the stalk. An *acrocephalic* person has a misshapen, *i.e.*, pointed skull. UFO is an *acronym* for an unidentified flying object.

2. **apo–**

   An *apologue* is a story told to point out a moral. Compare *apology*, something spoken from a need to be understood or pardoned.

3. **extra–**

   More than fifty words beginning with extra– are listed. One of the longest is *extraterritoriality*—nine syllables and nineteen letters.

4. **inter–**

   Of the more than 200 examples listed, the majority are familiar words.

5. **intro–, intra–**

   About two dozen words begin with intro– or intra–. One of the most familiar is *introduce*.

## BEYOND PREFIXES

1. **meta–**

   *Metonomy* is a good word to mention. *Metaphysics* is a philosophical term for the study of first principles and the nature of being or reality.

## 2. para–

Like meta–, para– comes from Greek and is usually attached to Greek roots. *Paramilitary* activity is carried on by persons *beyond* the regular military forces. Thus it is illegal, unauthorized, secret, or possibly semiofficial. *Paramount* comes from the Latin *per*; *parapet* from the Latin verb *parare* (to guard or shield). *Paradise* is ultimately traceable to peri– (around).

## 3. super–

An overworked prefix with well over one hundred "clients," it has a wide range, from dozens of self-defining words like *superimpose* to such sharply defined words as *superego*.

## 4. ultra–

This colorful prefix has a small family. Less than thirty words beginning with *ultra–* are listed in a college dictionary.

## 5. hyper–

The use of hyper– is mostly confined to technical terms like *hypertrophy* (abnormal enlargement of an organ or tissue). The same is true of hypo–. *Hypoglycemia*, for example, means too little sugar in one's blood. Sixty other hypo– words may be found in a college dictionary.

# SOMEWHAT SINISTER STEMS

## 1. –cide–, –cis– . . . –sect–

The root of –cide– is the Latin verb *caedere*, to cut or kill. Like *decision*, the words *precise, concise,* and *excision* are examples of –cis–, but *excise* (tax) comes from the Latin word *census*, a tax.

## 2. necro–

A *necropsy* is an autopsy, and *necrolatry* is worship or excessive reverence for the dead.

## 3. –pet–

Most words beginning with pet– come from different sources. The largest group is the petro– (rock) words, of which *petrify* (stiffen or turn to stone) is an example.

## 4. –press–

The root is *premere*, to press, from the past participle of which come *press* and the words listed in the text.

5. **–sperse–**

   *Sparge* (to splash or sprinkle) is occasionally seen.

6. **–turb–, –turbat–**

   The Latin root of *disturb* and *perturb* is *turbare*, to throw into confusion.

## WATER AND THE SEA

1. **–flu–, –flux–**

   *Effluence* (the flowing out of a stream or almost anything resembling a stream of water) may be added. The root is the Latin word *fluere*, to flow. *Efflux* and *effluvium* (outflow, noxious vapor or odor) are variants.

2. **–mari–, –marine–**

   Anything *marinated*, like herring, is soaked in brine, which is tantamount to sea water. *Marinade* has a similar meaning. The root of the "sea" words is the Latin word *mare*, sea.

3. **–naut–**

   *Nautilus* comes from the Greek word *naus*, a ship.

4. **–nav–, –navig–**

   A *navicert* is a document from a nation at war certifying that a ship of a neutral nation carries no forbidden material and should be permitted to pass through the enemy's blockade.

## KEYS

**First Practice Set**

| | | |
|---|---|---|
| 1. sea | 10. beyond | 19. outside |
| 2. dead | 11. beyond | 20. extreme |
| 3. killing | 12. flows | 21. cuts |
| 4. pressed | 13. sailors | 22. beyond/above |
| 5. from | 14. scatter | 23. upset |
| 6. tip | 15. troubles | 24. into |
| 7. among | 16. ships | 25. flowing |
| 8. attack | 17. converge | 26. too little |
| 9. extreme | 18. beyond | |

## Second Practice Set

1. above
2. (away) from
3. beyond/above
4. extremely
5. troubled
6. pushing/squeezing
7. flows
8. beyond
9. force
10. inside
11. beyond
12. excessive
13. beyond
14. between
15. within
16. under
17. beyond
18. sea
19. excessively
20. scattering, between

## Replacements

1. superfluous
2. nautical
3-4. dissecting ... incisions
5. homicide
6. interscholastic
7. hypercritical
8. marine
9-10. competitive, impetuous
11. confluence
12. Apocrypha
13. extraordinary
14. mariners
15. meteor
16. asperity
17. paradox
18. acronym
19. necromancy
20. repression

## Change of Pace

1. A college dictionary lists over 250 <u>inter–</u> words. Ten examples using relatively familiar roots are:

   | | |
   |---|---|
   | intercede | international |
   | intercontinental | interpersonal |
   | interdependence | interpose |
   | interference | interspersed |
   | intermission | intervention |

2. Examplers of *super–* words are:

   | | | | |
   |---|---|---|---|
   | superable | superintend | superpower | superstate |
   | supercilious | superior | superscription | superstition |
   | superfine | superjacent | supersede | supertax |
   | superheated | superlative | supersensible | supervene |
   | superhuman | supernatural | supersensory | supervise |

   Five <u>super–</u> words explained:
   supercargo—officer in charge of the cargo on a merchant ship
   superego—critical, moral aspect of the psyche
   supererogatory—uncalled for; done or observed beyond what is required or expected
   supernumerary—extra; superfluous; beyond a specified number
   superstructure—part of a structure above the ground or above the surface (in the case of a ship)

   A college dictionary lists over 150 <u>super–</u> words.

3. Variant forms of each –pet– word are:
petulant, petulantly, petulance
impetuous, impetuously, impetuousness, impetuosity
compete, competent(ly), competence, competition
repetition, repetitive(ly), repeat
*Appetite, impetus,* and *petition* have no familiar variants, but note that *petition* may function as either noun or verb.
The –petal in *centripetal* literally means search (for a center), *i.e.,* the force rushing toward or into the center that pulls a whirling object toward that point. (–Al is the adjective ending.)

5. Seven –press– words and their variant forms are:

| | | |
|---|---|---|
| compress | compressive(ly) | compression |
| depress | depressive(ly) | depression |
| express | expressive(ly) | expression |
| impress | impressive(ly) | impression |
| oppress | oppressive(ly) | oppression |
| repress | repressive(ly) | repression |
| suppress | suppressive(ly) | suppression |

Prefix opposites include *uncompressed, undepressed, unexpressed, unimpressed, unoppressed, unrepressed, unsuppressed.*

6. Among the –cide words not listed in the text are: *infanticide; insecticide; germicide; matricide; sororicide.*
*Aquacide* would doubtless be death by water, self-inflicted; yet, strictly speaking, it should mean destroying or doing away with a body of water. *Astrocide* would be the killing or destruction of a star, an improbable feat. An *aquanaut* would be literally a sailor on water. But the word is used to describe men who explore the ocean depths as *astronauts* explore space.

7. The prefixes may be explained thus:
*super*lative — an adjective carried beyond or above ordinary use to the highest intensity of meaning
*ultra*ism — extremism, the practice of being out beyond everyone else in fashions, tastes, ideas, or actions
*hyper*trophy — abnormal enlargement of an organ or tissue
*meta*bolism — the process of nutrition, both assimilative and decompositional: the process (–ism) of (nourishment) thrown or carried (–bol–) beyond (meta–)
*acro*polis — literally the foremost, actually the uppermost, part or tip of a city (–polis–) (Most cities had one.)
*super*cilious — literally, with eyebrows up or turned upward
*inter*mezzo — music written to be played between the acts of a play or parts of some other kind of presentation
*extra*legal — beyond or outside the law
*im*pressionism — a kind of art that gives the pictorial effects desired without precise detail

## Matching Set

1. 8
2. 4
3. 1
4. 11
5. 3
6. 10
7. 6
8. 12
9. 5
10. 7

## Unit Test  *(Word Wealth Testing Program)*

1. c (turbogenerator: power)
2. a (parasites: diseases)
3. a (turbulence: placidity)
4. d (supernatural: mundane)
5. b (Apocrypha: hidden books)
6. c (subaqueous: seas)
7. c (extroversion: introversion)
8. a (insensitive: hypersensitive)
9. b (acrogen: plant life)
10. a (clairvoyance: parapsychology)
11. b (disperse: gather together)
12. c (interpret: metaphors)
13. b (hyperacidity: low acidity)
14. a (necropolis: cemetery)
15. b (hypercritical: uncritical)
16. a (extensiveness: intensity)
17. b (extrapolation: mathematics)
18. c (genocide: nation)
19. a (turbulent: unpertubed)
20. c (influx: exodus)

# unit eight

## APPE-TEASERS

1. psychosis
2. orthodox
3. rectitude
4. carnivorous
5. chronological
6. corpulence
7. temporal
8. sentiment
9. spectral
10. sonic
11. tangent
12. verification
13. contemporaneous

## TO KNOW AND TO THINK

1. **–cog(n)– . . . –scien– . . . –gnos–**

   *Precognition,* a word from parapsychology for *prescience* (knowing beforehand what is going to happen) may be added. *Conscientious* is a –scien– word, and *gnomic* (wise and pithy) a –gnos– word. The root of –gnos– is the Greek word *gnosis,* knowledge, which comes in turn from *gignoskein,* to know.

2. **–doc–, –doctrin– . . . –dox–**

   In some universities, mostly abroad, a *docent* is a teacher who is not one of the regular faculty members. A *doctrinaire* person is unyielding and impractical in applying theories or beliefs.

3. **–ment–, –mem(or)– . . . –psych–**

   *Mental* and other –ment– words come from the Latin *mens, mentis,* mind. The –memor– words, including *memorable, memoirs, memory,* and *remember,* come from the Latin word *memor,* mindful. Numerous –psych– words are listed in the introduction to *Word Wealth* on p. xi.

4. **–morph–**

   The Greek root is *morphe,* form. *Dimorphous* (having two forms), *morpheme* (smallest unit of form and meaning in linguistics), and *Morpheus* (the god of dream forms) are a few additional examples.

5. **–pli– . . . –plic–**

   *Complicate, reply,* and *replicate* are additional examples. The root is the Latin *plicare,* to fold or weave.

## 6. pseudo–

A *pseudomorph* has a false or irregular form; or it may be a mineral which has the outer form and appearance of some other mineral.

## 7. –pute–, –putat–

All of the –pute– words come from the Latin verb *putare*, to think.

## 8. –rect– . . . –ortho–

Compare *rectangle, rectilinear, orthogenesis,* and other technical words of the life sciences using ortho–.

## 9. –temp– . . . –chron–

*Temper, temperance,* and *temperature* also come from the Latin verb *temperare*, to regulate.

## 10. –ver–, –verit–

From the Latin roots *veritas*, truth, and *verus*, true, come *aver* and *averment; very* and *verily;* and *veracity* (WW p. 55), but not *revere* or *severe*.

## 11. –vi–, –via–

*Viatic* (of a road or journey), *viaticum* (traveling expenses—or the Eucharist given to a person in danger of death), and *viator* (a traveler) are three rarely used offshoots of *via*.

# THE FIVE SENSES

## 1. –aud–, –audit–

An *audiometer* measures one's hearing; an *audiophone* is a hearing device; and *audio-frequencies* are sound frequencies below the audible limit of 20,000 cycles per second.

## 2. –sent– . . . –path–

*Resent*(*ment*) is another projection of the Latin verb *sentire*, to feel. A *pathogenic* agent is one that causes disease.

## 3. –son– . . . –phone–

Compare *sonar* (a high-frequency sound system used in submarine warfare) and *orthophonic* (a name for a sound system).

4. –spec–, –spect–, –spic–

*Inspect, prospectus, circumspect, perspective, specimen,* and *retrospect* may be added to the list, also *auspicious, perspicuous, perspicacity* (WW p. 200).

5. –tang–, –tact–

*Contingent* (happening by chance), *contingency* (possible complication or misfortune), and *intact* are additional members of the –tang–, –tact– word clan.

6. –vide–, –vis–

*Revise* and *revision* (but not *devise* or *division*), *advise* and *advice* (but not *invidious* [*envious*]) may be added to the list.

## BODY AND HANDS

1. –carn– . . . –sarc–

*Carnal* (living for worldly or sexual rather than for spiritual ends) is an older, half-archaic –carn– word, and *sarcology* is the anatomy of the soft tissues of the body. A *carnivore* is a flesh-eating (*carnivorous*) mammal.

2. –corp–

*Corpus Christi* (the body of Christ) and *corpus juris* (a collection of the laws of a country or district) may be mentioned. *Corporeity* is the state of being *corporeal*, *i.e.*, a word for bodily existence. *Incorporeal* beings are spirits; they do not have bodily form.

3. –man(u)–, –mani– . . . –chiro–

*Maneuver, mandate, manage,* and *manufacture* are derived from the Latin word *manus*, hand. *Chiropodist*, mentioned under –pod–, may be cited again. *Enchiridion* is a half-forgotten and rather superfluous Greek-derived word for *manual* (a Latin-derived word) or *handbook* (Old English origin).

## KEYS

**First Practice Set**

| | | | | | |
|---|---|---|---|---|---|
| 1. | unknown | 8. | touch | 15. | body |
| 2. | mind | 9. | way | 16. | see |
| 3. | think | 10. | shape | 17. | fold |
| 4. | hearing | 11. | bodies | 18. | truth |
| 5. | time | 12. | time | 19. | looks |
| 6. | right | 13. | feeling | 20. | teachings |
| 7. | sounds | 14. | look | | |

## Second Practice Set

1. incarnation
2. audible
3. chronology
4. orthodox
5. cognizance
6. supersonic
7. amorphous
8. incorporation
9. prognosis
10. resonant
11. incorporeal
12. chronic
13. obviate
14. antipathy
15. erect
16. implicate
17. manual
18. pseudonyms
19. spectacular
20. veracity

## Matching Exercise

A.

1. 4
2. 9
3. 6
4. 2
5. 8
6. 3
7. 12
8. 1
9. 5
10. 11

B.

1. 12
2. 5
3. 1
4. 8
5. 10
6. 11
7. 4
8. 6
9. 3
10. 9

## Unit Test  (Word Wealth Testing Program)

1. d (syllabic: voluminous)
2. c (misdirection: rectify)
3. b (incorporation: embodiment)
4. a (corpulent: emaciated)
5. b (orthography: spelling)
6. d (sentimentality: feeling)
7. c (docility: submissiveness)
8. c (replica: facsimile)
9. a (theoretical: practical)
10. a (reminisce: recollect)
11. c (verify: confirm)
12. a (precognition: telepathy)
13. c (inferential: perceptible)
14. b (dissonance: harmony)
15. b (Mr. Republican: epithet)
16. a (consonant: chirographic [script])
17. a (chronicle: verisimilitude)
18. b (theoretical: calculated)
19. d (reminiscent: prospective)
20. d (orthogonal: rectangular)

# unit nine

## CONTRASTS

1. panchromatic
2. amphibious
3. autopsy
4. neolithic
5. omniscient
6. malingerer
7. homogeneous
8. neologism
9. apprehensive
10. euphemism

## MORE PREFIX STUDY

1. **alter– . . . hetero–**

   *Alternative* as a noun and an adjective may be mentioned. *Alter idem* is a Latin phrase for another person of the same kind. Additional hetero– words that may be cited out of a total of fifty are *heteromorphic* (having a form other than the normal one); *heteronyms* (having the same spelling but different pronunciation and meaning); and *heterosexual* as opposed to *homosexual*.

2. **ambi– . . . amphi–**

   *Ambient*, from ambi– plus *ire*, to go, encompassing or surrounding, is an additional example. "*Ambient* marshland nearly cut off the army's retreat." Certain forms of life are *amphibiotic*, able to live in the water in one stage and on land in another stage of development. An *amphipod* has feet for swimming and other feet for use on land.

3. **auto–**

   The Greek root is *autos*, self. *Autogenous* vaccine is obtained from the patient's own body. *Autohypnosis* is self-hypnosis. Of the seventy or so auto– words in a college dictionary, *automat, autogiro, autograph,* and *autoinfection* may be mentioned.

4. **neo– . . . nov–**

   A *neoplasm* is an abnormal growth of tissue, such as a tumor. *Neoteric* means recent, newly invented or, as a noun, a person who accepts new ideas and practices readily.

5. **omni– . . . pan–**

   Compare *omnibus* (a bus with large capacity, or an oversized book containing a collection of some kind); *omnipresent* (WW p. 164 under *ubiquitous*); and *omnifarious* (consisting of many varieties), frequently replaced by *multifarious*. The pan– words total more than one hundred.

## 6. tele–

*Telex* is instant transmission of messages by teletypewriter to any part of the world. *Entelechy,* a philosophical term for complete actuality, has the same Greek root as *teleology.*

## 7. verd–, virid–

Compare *viridity* (freshness, greenness, verdancy), *viridescence* (turning green), and *viridescent.*

## 8. retro–

Compare *regress* with *retrogress.* The latter more often implies moving backward into an earlier or worse condition.

# ANTITHETIC PAIRS

## 1. bene– . . . eu–

*Benefice* (an endowed church office or its income) may be added. The *beneficiary* of a life insurance policy is the person selected to receive the proceeds.

### mal–

*Maladminister, malapros, malcontent, malefactor, maleficient, malfeasance,* and *malformation* are a few words that might be listed. *Malaise* (vague feeling of discomfort or uneasiness), *mal de mer* (seasickness), and *mal du pays* (homesickness) are French expressions using mal–.

## 2. magna–, magni–

*Magnolia* takes its name from Pierre Magnol, a French botanist.

### micro–

The root is the Greek *mikros,* small.

## 3. prim–

Compare *primate,* which may mean either an archbishop or a member of the highest order of animals.

### –termin– . . . –fini(t)–

*Coterminous* is often used of eras or areas which coincide. Thus a school district may be coterminous with the village boundaries.

**4.** **−don−**

The *donee* is the person who receives a gift.

**−prehend−, −prehens−**

The Latin root is *prehendere* or *prendere*, to take or seize.

**5.** **−cal(or) . . . −therm−**

An *isotherm* is a line on a map connecting points that have the same mean temperature.

**−frig− . . . −cryo−**

From the Latin root *frigere*, to be cold, comes also *frigorific* (freezing or cooling). From the Greek root *kryos*, cold, comes *cryolite* (a fluoride of sodium and aluminum so called because it is white and looks icy); *cryoscopy* (a method of determining the freezing points of liquids); and *cryostat* (an instrument to maintain the temperature at a very low level).

**6.** **homo−**

*Homily* (a moralizing lecture) may be traced to homo−, though a more immediate source is the Greek *homilia*, instruction.

**−misce−**

The Latin root of this element is *miscere*, to mix.

# KEYS

### First Practice Set

| | | |
|---|---|---|
| 1. early | 8. green | 15. heat |
| 2. very small | 9. far away | 16. end |
| 3. good | 10. cold | 17. irregular (casual) |
| 4. backward | 11. illness | 18. the same |
| 5. self | 12. all | 19. well |
| 6. different | 13. both | 20. everywhere |
| 7. new | 14. new | |

### Second Practice Set

| | | |
|---|---|---|
| 1. malign | 7. heterogeneous | 13. thermal |
| 2. microscope | 8. neolithic | 14. interminable |
| 3. miscellaneous | 9. magnate | 15. pantheon |
| 4. retroactive | 10. omnivorous | 16. amphibious |
| 5. homonym | 11. refrigerant | 17. autonomous |
| 6. verdigris | 12. innovation | 18. apprehend |

## Third Practice Set

**A.**

| | | | |
|---|---|---|---|
| 1. 12 | 6. 11 | | |
| 2. 6 | 7. 10 | | |
| 3. 1 | 8. 4 | | |
| 4. 9 | 9. 2 | | |
| 5. 3 | 10. 5 | | |

**B.**

| | |
|---|---|
| 1. 6 | 6. 3 |
| 2. 9 | 7. 5 |
| 3. 7 | 8. 10 |
| 4. 12 | 9. 2 |
| 5. 1 | 10. 8 |

## Family Connections

1. Word element listings:

| Numerical | Scientific | Physical | Sensory |
|---|---|---|---|
| mono– | –scien– | –pod– | –audit– |
| bi– | –helio– | –man(u)– | –vis– |
| tri– | –stell(a)– | –ambul– | –gust– |
| uni– | –sol– | –gastro– | –tang– |
| du– . . . duo | –luna– | –corp– | –aud– |
| | | –ped– | –vide– |
| | | –mani– | –aud– |
| | | –gastr– | |

## Literally Speaking

1. 4 ("a little body")
2. 1 ("swiftfoot")
3. 5 ("touching together")
4. 3 ("the body of the offense")
5. 2 ("to free one caught by the foot")

## Bonus

1. The more familiar pairs include:
   ambiguous—unambiguous
   ambivalent—unambivalent
   apprehensive—unapprehensive
   benevolent—unbenevolent
   comprehensible—incomprehensible
   defined—undefined
   finite—infinite
   homogeneous—unhomogeneous
   magnanimous—unmagnanimous
   primitive—unprimitive
   promiscuous—unpromiscuous
   retrogressive—unretrogressive
   terminable—interminable
   verdant—unverdant

2. The pairs are:
   benediction—malediction     homogeneous—heterogeneous
   benevolence—malevolence     progression—retrogression
   benefactor—malefactor       prospect—retrospect

3. The opposite of *cryotherapy* is *thermotherapy*.

4. The following examples may be cited:
   bear (animal); bear (carry)
   mine (possessive); mine (source of ore)
   fast (speedy); fast (abstinence from eating)
   bow (curtsy); bow (for arrows)
   mow (the lawn); mow (for hay)
   tear (from weeping); tear (rend)
   sow (grain); sow (female pig)
   lead (by the hand); lead (heavy metal)
   row (series in line); row (fight)
   bass (voice range); bass (fish)
   last (final); last (form for shoes)

## Unit Test  *(Word Wealth Testing Program)*

1. b (magnify:exaggerate)
2. a (euphemistic:pleasant sounding)
3. d (benefactor:malefactor)
4. d (malignant:cancer)
5. a (donation:theft)
6. a (orthodoxy:heresy)
7. c (malign:benign)
8. b (primitive:aboriginal)
9. a (paleolithic:primitive)
10. d (finite:eternal)
11. c (magnification:microscopy)
12. c (retrospective:prospective)
13. a (grassy:verdant)
14. b (hydroplane:amphibian)
15. a (promiscuous:miscellaneous)
16. c (pantomime:drama)
17. d (magniloquent:grandiose)
18. b (prospect:retrospect)
19. c (homogeneity:heterogeneity)
20. a (neologism:archaism)

# unit ten

## WORDS IN ORDER

1. magnanimity
2. concord
3. ephemeral
4. geology
5. vitality
6. pneumatic
7. lucid
8. aquatic
9. acrophobia
10. sacrosanct

## THE COSMOS AND THE CREATION

1. –cosm(o)–

   *Cosmopolite* (a world citizen) may be added to the list; also *cosmography* (the study of the structure of the universe).

2. –de(o)–, –de(us)– . . . –theo–

   *Dieu*, the French version of the Latin word for God (*Deus*), appears in *adieu* and also in the Spanish *adios*. *Atheism, monotheism,* and *polytheism* are further examples of –theo–.

3. –di(urn)– . . . –journ– . . . –ephem–

   *Dial, diet,* and *dietetics* come from the Latin word *dies*, day. *Hexaemeron* (the six days of the creation) is an additional derivative of the Greek word *hemera*, a day.

4. –helio– . . . –sol–

   *Helium* is so called because it was first discovered on the sun. Our solar system is *heliocentric*. A *heliotrope* is a flower so called because it turns to face the sun.

5. –luc– . . . –lumen–, –lumin– . . . –photo–

   *Elucidate, pellucid,* and *Lucifer* all come from the Latin root *lucere*, to shine. *Illuminate, luminary,* and *luminescence* derive from *lumen, luminis*, light.

6. –mort– . . . –thana–

   The Latin word –mort–, dead, appears also in *amortize* (WW p. 257) *mortgage, immortal,* and *mortify*.

7. –stell(a)– . . . –astro–

Usually the latter or Greek element in these pairs has fewer and in any case more largely technical examples than the Roman, but in this case astro– appears in *aster* (the flower), *asteroid* and *astral*, besides the four listed in the unit; –stell(a)– offers *stellate* (star-shaped), the name *Stella*, *stelliferous* (abounding with stars), *stellify* (to place among the stars), and *stellular* (bespangled with stars) as additional examples.

8. –vir– . . . –anthropo–

*Lycanthrope* (a werewolf), *anthropophagus* (man-eating), and *anthropomorphic* (human form) are additional words.

9. –vita–, –vi– . . . –bio–

*Vitamin* is another example of a word from the Latin word *vita*, life. Additional bio– words include *biogenesis* (theory that only life can generate life), *biography*, *biolysis* (destruction of life by bacteria), *biopsy* (microscopic study of a sample of living tissue), *antibiotics*, and *biosphere* (that part of the earth and air that contains life).

## THE FOUR ELEMENTS

1. –aqua–, –aque– . . . –hydr–, –hydro–

*Aquacade, aquatic,* and *aquamarine* may be cited as derivatives of the Latin word *aqua*, water. *Carbohydrate, anhydrous* (no water), *hydrology* (study or science of water), *hydromancy, hydrocephalous* (excessive fluid in the head), and *hydrography* (mapping of bodies of water) are additional examples.

2. –flagr– . . . –pyr–, pyro–

Compare *Pyrex, pyretic* (of or causing a fever), and *pyreheliometer* (to measure energy from the sun).

3. –pneumat–

*Pneuma*, a word for soul or spirit, is the Greek root *pneuma* transliterated into English.

4. –terr–, –terra– . . . –geo–

*Terrigenous* (earth-born) is a word instructive in form but rarely seen in print. *Geochronology* deals with the age of the earth and its materials.

# OUR ROLE IN THE COSMOS

1. **–ami(c)– . . . –phil(o)–**

   From the Latin word *amicus*, friend, come also *inimical* (unfriendly) and *amiable*. From the Greek word *philos*, friend, come a score of words as diverse as *Philadelphia* (brotherly love) and *philander*. *Philip* (horse-loving), *philanthropic* (benevolent), *philogyny* (fondness for women), *philology* (the love of learning or the study of literature), but not *Philistine*, come from this root.

2. **–amor– . . . –amat–**

   *Inamorata* is also a derivative of *amorare*, to love; and *amatory* also belongs to the progeny of the Latin word *amare*, to love.

3. **–anim–**

   That the Latin word *anima* and the Greek word *pneuma* both mean air, wind, or spirit has created a problem for translators of the Bible. In some cases it is not easy to know whether to translate the word as air or spirit.

4. **–cord– . . . –cardi(o)–**

   *Cordial*, as well as *cardioid* (heart-shaped) and *endocarditis* (inflammation of the inner walls of the heart cavities) will serve to illustrate the range of –cord–, –cardi(o)–.

5. **–ferv–, . . . –ard–**

   *Fervidor* (from *fervere*) was the eleventh month of the forgotten French Revolutionary Calendar.

6. **–fid–, –fide–**

   *Affidavit* and *fiduciary* (held in trust) also come from *fidere*, to trust.

7. **–pen– . . . –penit–**

   *Penance* and *impenitence* may be cited as further examples.

8. **–phobia–**

   *Ponophobia* (abnormal fear of dirt) and *xenophobia* (fear of strangers or foreigners) may be added to round out the entry.

9. **–sanct–**

   The Latin root is *sanctus*, holy. Compare *consecrate* and *desecrate*, which come from the Latin verb *sacrare*, to make sacred or holy.

# KEYS

**First Practice Set**

1. spirit
2. dead
3. trust
4. water
5. life
6. fear
7. day ... day
8. loving
9. friend
10. fire
11. heart
12. sorry
13. star
14. fires
15. stars
16. god
17. day
18. light
19. light
20. holy

**Surprising Interlude**

1. The root-prefix meanings are as follows:
    amphitheater—a place for viewing (*theater*) spectacles from both sides (amphi–)
    cosmetics—literally, skill in decorating, from the Greek *cosmos,* order
    cosmetology—the study or science (–ology) of skill in decorating (skin or complexion)
    cryometer—measuring device (–meter) for cold, *i.e.,* very low temperatures
    hydrophobia—abnormal fear (–phobia) of water (hydro–), a characteristic of the disease
    philander—to make love insincerely or irresponsibly
    geopolitics—world politics

2. Of the more familiar adjectives, the following may be listed:
    
    | | |
    |---|---|
    | discordant | unenamored |
    | immortal | unfervent |
    | impenitent | unflagrant |
    | inanimate | unheliotherapeutic |
    | infidel | uninterred |
    | nonluminous | unjournalistic |
    | nonpneumatic | unmagnanimous |
    | nonviable | unsanctimonious |
    | unamicable | unstellar |
    | uncosmopolitan | untheological |
    | undehydrated | unvirile |

3. *xenophobia*—unreasonable hatred or fear of foreigners or strangers
    *bataphobia*—excessive fear of passing near high buildings, fear of being at a great height
    *phonophobia*—abnormal dread of noise

4. *anthropology*—the study of man—races, traits, customs, institutions, myths, etc.
    *biogenesis*—the study of the origins of life, especially the theory that life comes only from living organisms and not from nonliving matter

5. Forms of worship include:
   bibliolatry—worship of books
   gyneolatry—worship of woman or women
   eugeniolatry—excessive concern about eugenic factors
   anthropolatry—worship of man; deification of a human being

**Second Practice Set**

1-2. flagrant . . .
     mortality
3. vitality
4. luminous
5. diary
6. philanthropist
7. heliolatry
8. penitentiary
9. misanthrope
10. sanctimonious
11. cardiac
12. territory
13. animated
14. astronomy
15. apotheosis
16. animosity
17. acrophobia
18. perfidy
19. cosmos
20. amicable
21. hydrology
22. stellar
23. Heliopolis
24. diffident

**Matching Exercise**

1. 9
2. 7
3. 11
4. 5
5. 10
6. 1
7. 2
8. 12
9. 4
10. 8

## Unit Test   (Word Wealth Testing Program)

1. c (geology: the earth)
2. b (aerial: birds)
3. a (agoraphobia: claustrophobia)
4. d (harmonious: discordant)
5. c (penitentiary: convicts)
6. c (sacrosanct: profane)
7. b (heliolatry: geolatry)
8. d (penology: criminals)
9. a (ardor: fervor)
10. a (deify: humanize)
11. b (mortal: undying)
12. b (aqueous: aquatic)
13. d (philatelist: stamps)
14. d (amative: amorous)
15. c (chimpanzee: anthropoid)
16. c (heart attack: earthquake)
17. b (Tennyson: poet laureate)
18. b (conflagration: holocaust)
19. d (luminous: unilluminated)
20. d (amity: amicability)

# Teacher's Notes

# Teacher's Notes

# Teacher's Notes

# Teacher's Notes

# Teacher's Notes

# Teacher's Notes